T0276294

# OPEN HOUSE

# ADVANCE PRAISE FOR THE BOOK

'When Piyush pens his thoughts, he is no different from how he is in person—simple, direct, insightful'—Anand Mahindra, chairman of Mahindra Group

'If there's one thing I've learnt in my five decades of experience, it's that to survive the test of time, one must keep innovating. One must know what the consumers want and then find ways to deliver that to them. Understanding the pulse of a consumer, and the market, takes years of experience. And to have a stalwart like Piyush Pandey pack it all into a book, makes it a must-read for any aspiring entrepreneur'—Harsh Mariwala, founder and chairman, Marico Ltd

'I firmly believe that collaboration and teamwork have no hierarchy. The true mark of a leader is one who applauds their team's efforts by acknowledging their skills and strengths. Through his writing style, he skilfully draws parallels between teamwork and cricket! Piyush's book amplifies the true spirit of being a team player and its importance in the dynamic and exciting world of advertising. A highly recommended book that is a perfect blend of self-introspection and experiences. A must-read for anyone looking to be a part of this industry'—S. Ramadorai, former CEO and MD, Tata Consultancy Services

'Piyush's ability to have an anecdote and an answer, in response to every question, even the ones out of syllabus, is thanks to the unabashed ease with which he asks questions, that most of us have but we don't ask. He's not afraid or ashamed to pose the seemingly innocent questions to the ones around him and I'm sure he's asking many more similar questions to himself, all the time. And therein lies his ability to answer whatever is thrown at him . . . with ease, an illustration and candour. May his tribe increase'—Harit Nagpal, managing director, Tata Play

'An encounter with Piyush is usually a "shaken and stirred" experience. It causes a rise in physical and intellectual energy levels and a somewhat disoriented "what was that again" feeling as you feel familiar, comfortable points of view being turned on their heads even as you try and stand firm in your previous conviction!
Imagine, now, a book that is like having a chat-fest and a think-fest with Piyush that traverses the gamut of "ships and sails and sealing wax—and why the sea is boiling hot—and whether pigs have wings".

It isn't the smart, 'one-liners' Piyush that you will engage with in this book, nor the boisterous raconteur Piyush, not even the persuasive ad man Piyush but the reflective, down-to-earth Piyush whose care to share is front and centre.

There are nuggets of wisdom, deep insights distilled from decades of amazing and diverse experiences, authentic opinions and unvarnished home truths expressed in his easygoing way; no questions asked are unanswered because they were too abstract or too pedestrian or too personal or too uncomfortable. It's Piyush unplugged. It's Piyush's well of wisdom that we get access to'—Rama Bijapurkar, author and marketing consultant

'Piyush Pandey embodies the art of storytelling. Over the span of his career, he has helped breathe life and soul into many brands with his deep understanding of what makes India tick and what inspires and ignites a spark in people. This book is his effort to lay bare the method behind his craft, the madness that keeps him alive and hungry for more, the passion and purpose that continue to drive him to be not just an ad man but a "world citizen". He calls the book a "khichri" of his thoughts, ideas, learnings and existential angst—this truly is comfort food for the mind and soul'—Shereen Bhan, managing editor, CNBCTV18

# OPEN HOUSE

## WITH

## PIYUSH PANDEY

**BUSINESS**
An imprint of Penguin Random House

PENGUIN BUSINESS

USA | Canada | UK | Ireland | Australia
New Zealand | India | South Africa | China

Penguin Business is part of the Penguin Random House group of companies
whose addresses can be found at global.penguinrandomhouse.com

Published by Penguin Random House India Pvt. Ltd
4th Floor, Capital Tower 1, MG Road,
Gurugram 122 002, Haryana, India

First published in Penguin Business by Penguin Random House India 2022

ISBN 9780670096671

Typeset in Sabon by Manipal Technologies Limited, Manipal
Printed at Replika Press Pvt. Ltd, India

www.penguin.co.in

*To Suresh Malik, with respect and gratitude.*
*Suresh was the national creative director of Ogilvy when*
*I joined as one of many young account managers in Ogilvy*
*Mumbai. He spotted a creative potential in me that I had*
*never thought of. Soon, Suresh and the late Mani Ayer*
*convinced me to switch from account management to*
*creative in 1987. Seven years later, when Suresh had to retire*
*early due to health issues, he handed over the responsibility*
*of the national creative director's role to me.*
*I owe everything that I have achieved as a creative*
*professional in advertising to Suresh.*
*Everything. RIP, Suresh, and thank you.*

# Contents

# Foreword

'When you're next in Mumbai I'll show you the bike that I've designed!'

Early 2001. Bajaj was months away from launching the Pulsar in an all-or-nothing gamble to transition from being India's Hamara Bajaj scooter to The World's Favourite Indian Motorcycle. We needed Indian advertising's Bhishma Pitamaha to put his creative shoulder to the wheel. One unforgettable morning, Piyush filled the room as he first walked into our Akurdi, Pune office with signature moustache, *mojris* and mirth in tow!

I clearly erred in placing before him not just the product's details but also my communication idea! This swiftly invited the retribution above telling me exactly where I stood and clearly indicated that I needed to stand right there! Which advertising professional would so dare meet the very first ball off the front foot on foreign soil demonstrating quiet confidence in his position while telling his 'partner'—as Piyush since refers to me in response to my addressing him as 'Sir'—to stay within his crease at the other end?!

It is for this intensely passionate ownership of his beloved craft that Piyush has since ascended to become the *vishwaguru* of advertising in his current avatar as chairman, Global Creative, Ogilvy. And it is with this unapologetically fierce yet unfailingly well-intended candour that he has in this *Open House* offered richly seasoned insights into issues ranging from relationships, careers, diversity and politics to consumer evolution, technology revolution, team building and institutional ethos.

Not only because he can but because that's his very DNA: to always borrow from life and to then give twice as much back.

You will relish his *Open House* for all of its multifaceted spaces.

First, for **fun spaces**. As a little boy Piyush once sneakily tied a length of twine to his toe, with the other end of the twine tied to a cricket ball that hung 20 feet below as he slept on the terrace so that when his friends yanked it early the next morning, he could quietly cycle off to a game in Ajmer without waking his father! As a young man at St Stephen's, he notoriously dug a hole through the neighbour's wall into the cupboard of a classmate who wouldn't share his goodies! And as a grown man he wickedly had the *durban* at Taj Colaba call into the porch the driver of a random car number so that he could park in the slot vacated! You will savour his 'tedi ungligiri' antics through this narrative!

Second, most obviously, for **creative spaces**. Legend has it that the secret sauce of Piyush's brilliance is a blend of his morning chai and his afternoon—even when in office!—siesta (during the lunch hour)! What else can explain his master stroke in sharply positioning the Bajaj Pulsar as being Definitely Male, thus cruelly repositioning all other motorcycles suitably?! He insists that the idea came to him when he repeatedly heard the refrain 'meri bike chalti hai' (in Hindi, a bike is a feminine noun); I suspect, though, that it wafted in on the morning mist or else infiltrated through in a midday dream! Throughout your *Open House* tour you will see seemingly familiar things like you've never seen them before, leaving you almost unknowingly wiser than you've ever been before.

Third, for **simple spaces**. Piyush adores his audience above all, and equally abhors burdening them to boredom with the 'gyan' of philosophy and weighing them down with the complexity of seriousness. His gift for boiling, distilling and straining any issue down to a singular, crystal-clean proposition that resonates with the street comes shining through page after page. Furthermore, it is not just this minimalistic but noble streak of simplicity in his persona that had him vociferously endorse his competitor's work that made the Bajaj Sunny an overnight sensation as the Simple Riding Machine. That, in turn, he tells me, became the proverbial springboard that catapulted the most talented Prasoon Pandey into a trajectory that has since led him into a league of his own.

Fourth, for **audacious spaces**. Piyush is neither dogmatic nor prescriptive, instead perpetually observing, reflecting, sharing and learning. For him evidence is necessary and hence important but experience alone is sufficient hence critical. He thus embodies the highest quality of accumulated excellence in thought given not just his extremely competitive nature that's feverishly egged on by his will to always win, but even more so, in my experience, by his deep desire to always think biggest. I found that to come to the fore when he led the launch of the Bajaj Discover in 2004 with the 'The Last Temptation' campaign, packing the team off to shoot with Jackie Chan in a Chinese monastery in the bitter cold and to an insanely unreal timeline!

Fifth, for **sensitive spaces**. Every instance that we have interacted, Piyush has warmly enquired about my father's well-being, and then shared with endearing affection updates of his incredibly large and enviously illustrious family. On each visit to Pune, he has graciously accepted my invite to stay at my home and spend the evening regaling and enlightening us. As I dogmatically labour in 'yogasanas', Piyush will spend hours playing with each of our five dogs—even calling upon Nita's (his wife, who works with dogs) services when they're unwell—and with my twenty-three-year-old son who will likely look back in awe twenty years hence. Piyush carries a sharp salute for every house help, and they wear their widest smiles for him. I reckon that indeed this acute sensitivity in him is the root of several innovative Ogilvy competencies such as their being the first to masterfully leverage audio, especially music, to distinctly embellish their most distinguished work. Thus, there is a certain air of humility and a spirit of gratitude that cannot but be sensed as you explore the show in his *Open House*.

Sixth, for the **loyal spaces**. How incredulous is it that Piyush should, post the most prestigious St Stephen's, do a three-year stint as a tea taster at Goodricke, Kolkata to honour the pact that he'd struck with best buddy Arun Lal to accept only those opportunities that were offered to them both? I'm hardly surprised after my histrionics about ten years ago when upon viewing a critical film I felt so dejected that I left office, drove home, called Piyush and bitterly complained that the mediocrity of the production had me feeling suffocated with anxiety. Four days later O&M exhibited an exemplary revision apparently carved out over forty-eight hours of non-stop editing by the boss himself. This is the sort of hands-on, ear-to-the-ground, walk-the-talk, leading-from-the-front example that inspires champion teams and fortifies venerable organisations. It is this gritty sportsmanship imbibed from the dusty Ranji Trophy pitches that compels him to uncompromisingly lay open his mind and heart to every reader who ventures into his *Open House.*

Seventh, and finally, for **Indian spaces**. All know well of Piyush's glorious global eminence, be it as an adman, awardee, juror, mentor or advisor. Few know that he's barely proud for himself, revelling far more in an Indian being on top of the creative world. Fewer still know that he did it on his own terms, for instance even contemplating passing up his current global charge if it meant having to move to New York; Piyush thereby made Mumbai the epicentre of global creativity. And only a select handful are privy to witnessing him hunt down a home-style Indian meal every single day from Porto to Buenos Aires, in the process deriving great pleasure from the rest of the family then eating humble pie at his table! Undoubtedly it is this 'India first but tadka lagake' obsession that spawned 'Mile Sur Hamara Tumhara' (for which he wrote the lyrics) in a period when Indian advertising was arguably being dominated by quasi-Western sensibilities. Think Cadbury's. Think Fevicol. Think Asian Paints. Think Vodafone. Think Chetak. And welcome to the Open House that's been built by potter Pandey with the magical 'mitti' of Hindustan.

As you can probably tell, I'm rather overwhelmed at the end of this twenty-year-long walk down the *Pandeymonium* path. Piyush once told me, 'The client always gets the advertising that he deserves.' Sir, I'm blessed to also get the advertising professional that I don't fully deserve. It is with this sense of self-preservation that I have a closing request to make of you. The next time you feel the urge to light up, please allow it to be—in your most favourite words—well left. In the second half of our innings, much hitting out of the park awaits our will and willow. Together we've got to take our game really deep and, who knows, life may even present us with a super over!

With love, respect, gratitude and every good wish.

(For certain inputs, my thanks to R. Balki, filmmaker and former CEO of Lowe Lintas and to Kinu (Abhijit Avasthi), founder of Sideways Consulting).

Rajiv Bajaj,
Managing Director, Bajaj Auto

ॐ

# Introduction

I thought, in an impulsive moment, I would call my second book *Chajju ka Chaubara*. An explanation is required here. Chajju Bhagat was a religious leader, based in Lahore, during the reign of emperor Shah Jahan. A highly successful man, he conducted his affairs from a *chaubara*, an open house or

four-walled room that had windows and doors on all sides. His disciples and followers could enter from any direction and consult Chajju, reputed for his wisdom, on all manner of things. Chajju patiently answered all their questions.

I'm not a religious leader, nor do I claim to have wisdom beyond what a normal human being has. I don't have disciples or followers and cannot share thoughts on issues outside my personal experiences.

So, as we do in advertising, I threw the idea of the title into the dustbin and moved on. However, there is an element of the open house in the life of any successful person in advertising. When I first read about Chajju, I loved the idea of unrestrained access to his chaubara. Forget the chaubara for a moment and think about advertising. Now imagine a four-walled room with doors on all sides; imagine that anyone can walk in and share, criticize and improve upon ideas.

When I sat down with my curator, Anant Rangaswami, once again to write this book, we decided to attempt to create a virtual open house.

It's been six years since *Pandeymonium*, my book on my career, was published. Only six years.

During the past year, a number of friends egged me on to write a second book. It made no sense to me. After all, what had happened in these six years that was different and interesting to the reader?

I tried to think of what I had not covered in *Pandeymonium*. I thought about my colleagues, I thought about Ogilvy and WPP, and I thought about the brands and marketers I had worked with.

There was not much that hadn't been covered, either by the media over the years or in *Pandeymonium*. It made no sense to write a second book. But wait.

I thought about the chance meetings at airports and airplanes, and hotel lobbies with people I had never met earlier and about the questions they asked me. I thought about the questions from students at colleges where I was invited to speak and about the ones from delegates at conferences I was addressing. In a way, we were in an open house, where anyone could approach me from any direction and ask my opinion on cabbages and kings. However, unlike Chajju, I often did not have the time to answer these questions in detail as they would have liked.

Many of these questions caught me off-guard for their simplicity and directness. And these were the ones that were the most difficult to answer, but these needed to be addressed in all seriousness and with no time limitation.

If *Pandeymonium* was a collection of my thoughts on my career at Ogilvy, what if the second book was, simply, answers to questions from literally anywhere?

We invited, through social media and a press release, questions that anyone, anywhere wanted my answers to. Those were then put together in this book. These are the questions asked in a chaubara and the responses are merely my thoughts, not wisdom or advice.

So, in a way, this is your book, not mine.

Enough of the preamble. Now let's get to your questions, and to my answers. The book is not laid out as hundreds of answers to hundreds of questions, though. I've clubbed together questions that largely have common themes and arranged the answers as sort of 'essays'.

One stark difference, because of the questions, between this book and the previous one is that it's less anecdotal, and more introspective and based on my experiences.

I have attempted to create some order, and even answered questions that were completely 'out of syllabus' as there was no way to club them.

So, the book is a bit of a khichdi, which is the common food for thought. I hope it's good khichdi—khichdi that's been cooked in your open house.

# PART ONE

PART ONE

# 1

# Advertising Is a Team Game

Is advertising a good career option today?
How does one get into advertising?
How do I create so much?
What are the qualifications to do well in advertising?

Not surprisingly, many young people want to know more about the business of advertising, about advertising as a career, about how they could get into this field and excel in the field. While I continue to refuse to be prescriptive, I've shared my thoughts based on all that I've seen in the nearly forty years that I've been in advertising.

There are several questions that often come up. What are the educational qualifications that are required to get into advertising? How do I join advertising? Is advertising a good career choice? How do you create so much?

Answering these seemingly simple questions is more difficult a task than is apparent (I urge all my peers to try and answer them as well. Their response will be an education, even to me).

The understanding of 'advertising' has changed over the years; in the post-digital age, the change is both frenetic and continuous. When I joined advertising in 1982, you had to be a good thinker or an 'ideas' person or a good writer, a good art director or someone with a good sense of media (of those times), one with an understanding of what public relations entailed and so on.

If we look at the purpose of advertising, it is to craft a message, carry it to consumers and influence how they feel about the brands that we work for. When I began my career, these pieces of communication messages were created for television, radio, film, print, outdoor. That was the sum and substance of advertising. The qualification that was required to craft these messages was not complex and pretty easy to define, as I've attempted to do earlier in the book.

Times, however, have changed over the years. In today's world, advertising has many more needs and demands. As the mediums have expanded, so have the skill sets required to craft messages for these mediums. In addition to traditional media, brands now talk to consumers through digital media, social media, experiences, brand ambassadors, influencers, branded content, gaming and podcasts, among other things. The use of technology, especially in Augmented Reality and Virtual Reality, is increasing. Even someone technologically challenged like me can now initiate a Zoom call, log onto a Microsoft Teams call and so on because it is no longer viable for a professional to shun technology. While on this subject, when I think of AR and VR, the word that I focus on is 'Reality', not Augmented or Virtual. It keeps ideas in focus and allows the outcome to be more real. Media consumption habits for young consumers, particularly, are very different from the habits of even two decades ago and are changing rapidly. If TikTok has been banned in India, consumers of the app quickly find an alternative and migrate there. With these changes, all of us in advertising need to stay abreast of the changes and sometimes anticipate the changes.

Advertising has always found the consumer on the media that the consumer uses. If, in my early days in the business, media consumption was limited to what we now call 'traditional' media, it's changed dramatically now. With these changes, the qualifications required for a career or for growth in advertising have changed as well. The first requirement, which is non-negotiable, is that you need to be passionate about communication. Thereafter, you could be an engineer, (which was very rare in the old era of advertising, but very welcome with the role of technology and of digital today) you could be an art person, you could be a writer, you could be a history student, you could be anything; you could even be a chef. As long as you are passionate about communication and have any of these skills in addition, the world of advertising will welcome you with open arms. Despite the courses on advertising being offered by many reputed institutions, I'm firmly of the belief that there is no specific qualification that is needed by this industry—except a passion for communication. So much for the formal qualifications required.

Furthermore, you might wonder if it is an advantage if you come from a large city and a disadvantage if you come from a small town. Is it a strength if you can speak Hindi and a weakness if you cannot? Advertising needs all of you. From any corner of the country and speaking any language that consumers speak in. Advertising, in fact, needs the diversity; truly needs it—diversity of region, of languages, of tastes in every field, of gender, of age, of caste, creed, religion and empathy. The reason for this is that the most important element in advertising is that it is a team game: the more varied and complementary the skills in the team are, the better the result.

Many newcomers and aspirants come into this business dreaming of creating a great TV commercial or a print ad that appears on the front page of the daily newspapers or of the next 'viral' campaign on digital and social media. None of these is created by one person. None. In my nearly four decades in the business, I cannot name one single piece of work that has been created by an individual. Not one. That's why diversity is so important; you need a variety of skills, thoughts and opinions to succeed not just in the business of advertising, but to create a single ad. I've drawn a lot in my career from my experiences in a team sport, cricket specifically. You first join the team, but only as a single player, one of many in the team. Then you get the opportunity to play to your skills and, perhaps, if you perform well, you become famous.

What many miss out on is that unless you are a part of a team that becomes famous, there's very little chance of a player in the team becoming famous. If Bedi, Prasanna, Chandrashekhar and Venkataraghavan became famous, it is because of the performances of their teammates (the close-in fielders like Solkar, Abid Ali and Surti, for example, and the batsmen like Gavaskar, Vishwanath and Sardesai, for example, and Farokh Engineer, the wicket-keeper) that the team became a winning team. Fame and adulation are by-products of this success. You become a hero by being a part of the team that's the bigger hero. There's little joy in being named the man of the match when playing for the losing side; the fame is both shallow and short-lived.

While we discuss building a team, let me address some related questions as well.

# How does a young candidate who is not from a big, recognized, famous college make a mark? How do they get a job in the big agencies?

Every company is interested in finding good people—wherever they might come from. Some of them get hired through the obvious and common formal recruitment processes (through the HR department, and so on), but hiring is not done by these processes alone. Formal processes are required because there are multiple candidates and many aspirants; one needs to find a way to make recruitment more efficient. But there must be avenues of identifying the oddball; there must be avenues for chancing upon candidates like me. As I've said earlier, the qualifications for a career in advertising are sort of undefined except for a passion for communication. I had nothing when I walked into Ogilvy except for the passion, and there are many more like me around the world. There have been hotel management students who made it bigger than me, there have been metallurgic engineers who made it to the level of creative director, and a few of them would have been noticed through the formal process. David Ogilvy was a chef; Andy Main (global CEO, Ogilvy) used to sell potatoes door-to-door.

If we don't keep a window open to allow the entry of talented and passionate individuals beyond the process, we will be the losers.

Few agencies look for big names of colleges when assessing talent. If you're passionate enough about this business, you will find a way to cut through the clutter and get yourself noticed.

It's in the context of advertising being a team game that I answer questions that a few of you have asked me about Neil French.

If one looks at Neil through the filter of 'qualifications required for a job in advertising', he would have ticked all the boxes. He was passionate about advertising and communication, and supremely talented as a writer. As long as Neil was at Ogilvy, he was a star. He went on to join Michael Ball as a partner at The Ball Partnership, a then new age company that attracted many other talented professionals, including our very own (late) Ranjan Kapur.

What went wrong with The Ball Partnership when it was bursting with talent? My answer is an answer of someone watching from the sidelines, with no first-hand experience of the developments. I try and figure out what happened. Neil French was an extraordinary creative based out of Singapore, and you have to understand Neil, his achievements and career in a context. He and his team focused on an English-speaking, print-consuming audience in Singapore, but his ability to communicate in the English language was able to transcend Singapore and be relevant to most English-speaking markets. In addition to being a great writer, he was an extraordinarily talented art director. He chose, early, the opportunity in creating disruptive and shocking campaigns (I use the word 'shocking' in a positive way) that got him and his work noticed. His work saw him grow to becoming the head of creative of Ogilvy and, indeed, of WPP, the network. He managed to make a place for himself as one of the greats of advertising. And then he went on and joined The Ball Partnership. The talent that Neil had remained, the reputation that he had built aided him, the ability to create disruptive work never left him. Yet, The Ball Partnership was short-lived. Why? This is because advertising is a team game. Michael Ball and Neil French fell out, and, at the very minimum in a team game, if it's a twosome, they have to tango. I'm not given to gossip, so I guess we will all have to wait for either Michael or Neil to tell us what transpired. To my mind, the business failed because of another element in the team game—the institution that houses the players. I don't think Michael (perhaps because of his age when he launched The Ball Partnership) wanted to build an institution and all that it entails. Institutions take a long-term view of profits, losses, philosophy and their people. As a consequence, those involved take a long-term view of each other, which automatically forces one to take an attitude of a bit of give-and-take.

In my career, I had to deal with Ogilvy's views, with views from my colleagues such as Ranjan Kapur or Rane or Kunal Jeswani or Madhukar Sabnavis, Premnarayan, Hebzibah Pathak or my creative leaders Kainaz Karmakar, Harshad Rajadhyaksha and Sukesh Nayak. We don't agree all the time on all issues, but the larger institution around us makes us debate opposing views in an atmosphere of healthy mutual respect. My guess is that there were pulls and pressures that Neil and Michael disagreed on, and, in the absence of an institution to 'belong' to, the company collapsed under its own contradictions. Neil and Michael were both stars when they started The Ball Partnership. What they missed, perhaps, was a team to belong to.

As in any team sport, it's a nightmare if everyone in the team is a star, if everyone wants to be the captain. You cannot have a cricket team with eleven opening batsmen only, even if each one of them is as talented as Sunil Gavaskar. You need top-order batsmen, the middle order, the bowlers, the wicketkeeper and the fielders.

Cricketing analogies are easy to create and easy to understand (except for the few in the US who might read this). In any team game, you need the contribution of every single team member. A few of these members will become famous, will be seen as stars, but each one needs to contribute. It took Balwinder Singh Sandhu (hardly a big name in the team) to bowl the brilliant ball that flummoxed Gordon Greenidge in the 1983 Prudential World Cup. I like the recognition of the 'assist' in football nowadays, in addition to the recognition of the goal-scorer. But take a solo sport like tennis. Roger Federer, seemingly, is alone. But behind him, unseen and unnoticed, is a team of over fifty professionals—trainers, coaches, doctors, masseurs, psychologists—who ensure that 'team Federer' wins. Similarly, in advertising, too, there are stars who capture the headlines because they 'score goals'. But behind each of these scorers is a galaxy of enablers, and the role of the enabler is as important as the role of the scorer.

### Who is your favourite cricketer?

Some answers have to come from the heart, not from statistics. My favourite cricketer since my childhood is Sir Vivian Richards. He continues to be my favourite cricketer.

To me, he embodied raw energy. The smile on his face, whatever the situation, underlined his pure love for the game. To me, he never looked like a professional cricketer; he was someone who loved the game and happened to do so well at it that he turned professional.

His swagger as he walked up to the crease or as he fielded. His delight when he connected sweetly with the ball or took a catch to dismiss the batsman; greater delight when he took a wicket as a bowler and his unconcealed pride in playing for the West Indies.

The way that he could change the game and dominate it completely by improvising, not with the shots that we see in the T20 matches today, but using textbook stroke were a joy to behold.

I had the opportunity to see him bat in the New Delhi test in 1974, only his second test in Test cricket, when he scored an unbeaten 192 runs. In those days, we could afford only the cheapest tickets, but I would go to the stadium at 6:30 a.m. to find the best view from the cheapest seats and park there.

In that test, Viv Richards batted like a man possessed, accumulating runs against the best spin combination in the world—Bedi, Prasanna and Venkatarghavan.

Thank you, Viv, even if India lost that test by an innings.

His swagger is forever imprinted in my mind. It was a swagger created by self-belief, confidence, performance and joy for the game.

Perhaps unconsciously, it's a swagger that slowly crept into Ogilvy India's body language.

By coincidence, in 2019, Ogilvy and I had the opportunity to be involved in the launch of his daughter Masaba Gupta's innovative clothing line 'I will wear out plastic' which was designed to allow the clothes to be repurposed as shopping bags and thus cut down the usage of plastic.

One part of me was delighted to have any fresh connect with the man I admire so much, Sir Vivian Richards.

The client-facing or media-facing colleagues, whether in creative or other areas, look like stars or as bright as the moon. The moon, which is fed by the light of the sun. Without the rays travelling to the stars and to the moon, these would be unseen and unheralded. The colleague who serves you tea when you're working at 2 a.m. is enabling you to write campaigns. A colleague in client servicing who's providing you with information, or planners who provide you with insights or literally (and this is hugely important) *any other person*, young and old, who can make one single little point which sparks off an idea in you, is a part of the team. These colleagues will not become famous instantly because of the little idea that they articulated or the tea that was served and helped provoke or enable a big idea or campaign. The media-facing and client-facing professionals become famous. David Ogilvy famously said, 'Some of the best ideas come from account executives, researchers and others. Encourage this; you need all the ideas you can get.'

'Har ghar kuch kehta hai' (loosely translated, 'every home has something to say about the occupants') for Asian Paints was an idea sparked by my colleague Madhukar Sabnavis, my planning colleague and currently vice-chairman of Ogilvy India but because he chooses to be under the radar, it's his media-facing colleagues who get the credit.

To dismiss or underestimate the roles and contributions of the others by those who become famous is both irresponsible and dangerous to their own future work.

Let me illustrate this. In April 2020, during the early days of the pandemic, my team had me on a call to discuss a campaign that would encourage the wearing of masks. My wife Nita, who used to work in advertising, said, 'Why don't you look at children and the way we ask them to "behave" and not expose their backsides when their shorts are falling off? Adults and children alike say "shame, shame" when we see an exposed bum.'

So, is there an idea there? The next day my team and I explored this thought; eventually, we settled on another approach. But, if we had continued down the 'shame, shame' route, does one forget where the glimmer of the idea came from? This was a personal experience, but it happens in office all the time.

During a brainstorming session, someone innocently says, 'you might want to look at it this way'. Or someone else chips in with, 'I'm sorry, it may sound like a bad idea, but I thought . . .' And often, it's not a bad idea. It's a great idea. Youngsters and freshers may not feel confident to say it's a great idea. Very few creative directors can call an idea a 'great' idea as it is being developed, and that includes me. But with experience you can recognize a good idea and have the understanding on how to develop the good idea into a possible great idea. What does this translate to? That the germ of the idea could be from anyone in the team, even those just 'passing by'. I have so many colleagues who work behind the scenes and about whom you never read about in the media, and many of them are the originators of the greatest ideas that you credit to the 'famous' and the 'stars'.

There's a place in the sun for everyone. Everyone plays their part. In these forty years, I've moved from a trainee to a client-servicing executive to a member of the 'Hindi' department to a creative director to a CEO to a chairman and now to a global role. Whatever the designation, I had to be a member of a larger team.

Several of you asked about my current role and whether it has hampered my 'creativity. The role of any leader, in this case a Global CCO (and, as this is being edited, I'm now redesignated chairman, Global Creativity) is, fundamentally, leading a team. And continuing in the same vein of the cricket analogy, here's how I would describe it.

I'm a playing captain of the team along with my partner Joe Sciarotta; I'm not the manager of the team, not the enforcer of rules. I have to respect the team. I took on the role as global CCO only on 1 January 2019. In 2021, I was given a new role and designation as chairman of global creative in addition to my India-focused role. I have attempted to learn from the examples of the great global CCOs I've worked with, including David Ogilvy. Fundamentally, they have tried to recognize talented professionals who understand the audiences in the geographies that they live in and proceed to work with them as partners. There can be little doubt that a creative director in Sao Paulo or in London will know the people, habits, languages, idiom and cultures in their offices far better than I ever could. You begin with a large dose of respect for the work they do and for the understanding they have, and then your role is limited to team-building and encouraging sharing of great ideas and best practices. The role of a global CCO is not the role defined by a hierarchy. I'm not the boss. It is the role of a world citizen. A world citizen who respects every country, and the country heads, no matter what discipline they come from.

If the role hampers my creativity, then I'm not fit for the job. Because if I have to encourage my colleagues and be the enabler of champions of creativity, I had better be creative myself. I'm a playing captain. The members of the team expect me to contribute positively. I cannot be scoring zeros and believe that I would remain the captain. There's a change in the role of a creative person as you grow older and get greater responsibilities. You have to be able to recognize the talent in the team, promote the deserving and their ideas, encourage them, reward them. In the process you have to look after them and keeping the team intact. That is the creativity that I'm consumed by in this role.

In the context of my current role, and in the context of advertising as a 'mobile' career, a few asked about the opportunities and challenges in moving out of your own country to regional or global roles.

There is no one-size-fits all answer to this. I've already spoken about Neil French and Michael Ball who made a name for themselves in Singapore, a country that was thousands of miles away from their roots.

There are some people who adapt well to every geography that they go to, and Neil was certainly one of them. Neil wasn't alone; there are many like him. At Ogilvy, we had an Australian, Barry Owens, who had settled down in Thailand. He assimilated so beautifully that he was almost Thai in his thinking and behaviour. He understood the country, the people, the language, the food, the music, the colours. As a result, he did some fantastic work and oversaw some fantastic campaigns created for Thailand, all created in Thai. Barry encouraged his team of Thai colleagues to express their own culture and their own ideas in their own language, but with Barry ensuring that the messaging was professionally done.

There will be many like Barry, capable of 'becoming' local and loving a new geography. But to those of you who think of leaving your home country and returning at a later date, I think it's important, in this fast-changing world, that you do not lose touch with the constant changes in the country that you want to return to.

Take a leaf from the book of the late Ranjan Kapur, my colleague, boss, partner and mentor, who worked for so many years outside India. While he was away he kept in close touch with India, making regular visits, so that when he came back as the managing director in January 1994, he was completely in tune with the recent changes in the Indian consumer landscape. If you lose touch with your home country and attempt to return, the many years of experience in an alien market will not matter much. When you explore

options abroad, think about it very hard. If you're like Barry and can adapt to a new geography and culture, it works. Or if you're like Neil French, who created ads not so much for a geography as for those who loved the language, it works. Or if you're like Ranjan, who invested constantly in staying abreast of the land that he was clear that he would go back to, it works too.

# 2

# Selecting Winning Teams and Retaining Them

How do you find partners?
How do you find team players?
How do you form a team?
How do you hold on to them?
How do you cultivate them?

If advertising is a team game, it raises many questions on how one makes a mark in the field. So how do you find partners? The truth is that people find you before you find them. It's your work that attracts people. It's my job, in all the roles where I've been responsible to hire team members, to try and meet as many candidates as possible because you never know where the spark will come from or be found. And you don't identify them purely by the business school or the art school that they went to, or any other technical college that studied at. You meet them, you talk to them about their skills, and get your colleagues who are capable of assessing the skills you might not have, into the conversation.

Once you get the competence out of the way, it is time to assess for attitude, passion and a sense of self-belief and self-assurance. I look for passion in the candidate, not the ambition to be a star in three years. The passionate will do the work and may or may not become a star. If you have a career path already plotted in your mind, then you will do things that you already planned step by step. And there is no step-by-step or pre-determined growth trajectory in advertising. The career growth happens from one milestone to another milestone. You score a century by scoring ones and twos, and fours and sixes; every ball cannot be a six. Self-belief and self-assurance are important in assessing the ability to communicate with team members because if you're going to communicate with the world, you must first learn to integrate with your partners. And believe that *we* have to win the match and not that *I* have to win the match.

A sense of security is critical in any form of business. In advertising, an insecure individual is incapable of sharing a raw idea or of contributing to improving a colleague's idea. What if, as a bowler on the cricket field, your fielder is insecure about your success and doesn't hold on to a catch? Or, as a footballer, a talented colleague doesn't want to pass the ball to you when you're in a scoring position due to his insecurities? So, it is best to stay secure and work towards becoming more and more secure within yourself. Pocket your ego and play for the team and when the team wins, that will give you the fame you want. Fame is not for you to acquire; it is to be earned. This is what has worked for me since my early days in advertising.

And having found the team members and having created the team, we come to the next set of challenges.

# How do you retain the members of your team? The team is ambitious, and they want to go somewhere, perhaps to a weaker team where they can shine . . . How do you hold on to these talented, but unhappy colleagues?

The cardinal rule of a team game is the need for all the players to have mutual respect for each other. Think of cricket; a debutant needs the support of all the senior team members to be able to excel in a game where he's selected to play in. Think of Sachin Tendulkar in 1989, making his debut against Pakistan at the age of sixteen. You cannot treat a junior member who's a playing member of your team as an insignificant player. They're a member of your team and carry equal weight. They might be less experienced, perhaps having won fewer titles or trophies, but they are still members of the same team.

Therefore, you have to treat them as equal team members; you have to be sensitive to their needs and concerns. Even the most talented professionals have some weaknesses and insecurities, and as the captain, it's your job to help them address or overcome the weaknesses, and make their talent come to the fore. Along the way you try to make them more confident members of the team and ensure that they contribute to the performance of the team. When they're an active part in a winning team, it's fairly easy to retain them. Winning football teams in the Premier League or La Liga, for example, find it easy to retain most players. When it comes to people wanting to do other things, you have no hold over them. All professionals have their own ambitions, their own passions. You can only share with them what you've learnt from the many instances in your life, and explain that these are the pros and cons. When I'm faced with such a situation (when some valuable team member has expressed that they want to leave), I've sat them down and shared the experiences that I've been through. My conversation with them probably helps them evaluate the possible scenarios before them a little better. Despite these attempts, if they're clear that they want to move on and have a clear path defined, I give them a hug and wish them the best for the future, possibly even helping them in their new role if it's not conflicting with my business.

When you ensure that the parting is done with mutual respect, the 'leavers' become goodwill carriers and your brand ambassadors for life. There are many who have left us, experimented and returned to O&M after a few years.

One has to facilitate the return and not burn bridges. Keep in touch when they leave, help them when they need it, and create a route for them to return happily and securely. Of course, there are some who leave and join a competitor, and do well there. If I take you back to sport, it's completely common for opponents to be good friends. You play a game against each other in the day and have a beer in the evening. Vivian Richards and Ian Botham fought fierce battles on the cricket field and were (are!) inseparable off the field. There are hundreds of such cases in every field even in politics. It is common for politicians to fight bitter battles in parliament or during elections, but, when the day is done, they cease being politicians and are happy in the company of friends from the opposition parties. This is true for advertising as well.

Talking of teams, I've received a few questions about team members who don't perform, team members who are troublemakers. How do these non-performers and troublemakers continue to stay in organizations and, often, keep rising up the ladder? How are these individuals not seen for the negative contribution to the company and the team?

Here's the short answer: troublemakers and wrong doers are fired on the spot. Non-performers are given a few chances and guidance before the company decides that they do not fit in with the Ogilvy way of working. It's the job of the management, at every reporting level, to spot them and deal with them. If they're not identified, those in charge are failing in their role. The impact of failure of managers to identify non-performers and allow them to rise in the organization has dangerous long-term consequences—the most important one being the loss of morale of the others in the team, particularly the performers. That's why one takes great care in choosing the leaders of the team. Choose the leaders well and the non-performers, in most cases, will have nowhere to hide.

# 3

# Creating a Company Aligned to Creativity

How do you build an ecosystem around a product using
creativity and marketing?
How can you build an audience tightly integrated with
the brand?

I jump now from creating a winning team that creates advertising to creating a company where every single member is aligned to the same extraordinary goal of creativity. Let's take the example of Apple. How does Apple build an ecosystem around its products using creativity and marketing? How is it able to build an audience so tightly integrated with the brand? I must say that while Apple indeed is extraordinary, there are many other companies that have done reasonably well in building a company, products, brands and communities. Off the top of my head I could name Nike, Coke, Burger King, Mondelez and, closer home, Pidilite and Asian Paints. Perhaps Google would be another. In each of these instances, the principles are the same.

Apple's employees, anecdotally, love going to office. They are free to express themselves and seem unhampered by rules and structures. Yet there is a system that brings together the culture and helps steer the company towards excellence; it's not that it's a free-for-all. What these companies have done is that they have managed to create an environment of creativity seemingly freed from constraints to express oneself. In most companies, for example in network agencies and other communication companies, rules and procedures are created to prevent chaos or deal with the unpredictable. Apple, from the time it began with the 1984 release of the Mac to the second journey under Steve Jobs, was unsatisfied with the normal or staid—it wanted extraordinary products and took extraordinary punts in the quest for these extraordinary products. The success with the iPod gave them the courage to invest more in experiments and take newer risks. The products that followed ensured that success.

Companies such as Apple spend an extraordinary amount of time and money in creating the culture that fosters out-of-the-box thinking. We admire the company because of the repeated successes that it has had. And we will continue to admire it since it continues to succeed. The product basket, owing to the near monopoly market that it enjoyed in the early stages, saw it reaping high margins, which in turn allowed it to invest in the next big idea.

Such companies are almost like close-knit families. The rules exist but are unwritten and unsaid. However, the 'ecosystem', the family is, as a collective, aware of problems, unhappiness and challenges that particular members of the family might be experiencing.

A critical part of the ecosystem are the partners of the business; they're also family and need to be treated as such. The role that Lee Clow and TBWA Chiat Day played in the success of Apple has been described many times by Jobs himself. Apple has worked with Lee's team since its inception. These are unusual cases, but visionaries like Jobs chase their dreams and do not bow to the pressures of the stock market. That allows them to take a long-term view of their product portfolio and their brand—something very few individuals have the courage to do.

I've had the pleasure of working with some brands for over twenty, thirty, forty years. The ones that easily come to mind are Fevicol, Asian Paints, Cadbury Dairy Milk and many Hindustan Unilever (HUL) brands. Other companies which have invested in their partners becoming long-term 'family members' include Amul. The performance of these brands is visible for everyone to see.

Can another Apple be born? Only if there is another Steve Jobs. Is Tim Cook the new Steve Jobs? That answer will help us understand if there is indeed an ecosystem that can win every time, or whether it was the vision of Steve Jobs that created the brand Apple is today. Apple's performance post the passing of Steve Jobs suggests that there is, indeed, an ecosystem that works.

# 4

# Good Talent Can Come from Anywhere

What about different career paths in advertising?
Is it possible to make your name in a small agency and go to
a large agency?
How to spot and hire good talent, and how not to?
What are the things you should take care of when you have
identified good talent and you're trying to get the talent
on board?

I receive many questions about first jobs in advertising. The early days often shape the future and freshers worry about whether or not they are making the right choices. They are never quite sure what the role is, and what is expected of them. This is truer in smaller agencies, where there is less structure, hardly any formal induction process and so on. In smaller agencies, client servicing is almost a euphemism for new business development. A young man who plays the guitar (and believes he has no other skills) is designated as a client-servicing executive, wondering whether he had a future in advertising. You could replace this young man and a guitar with almost any other combination. It could be a young lady and her love for poetry or another young man with a flair for cooking. All these combinations are good for a career in advertising, as long as you have the basic pre-requisite of a passion for communication.

There's no agency that can ever exist without a client relationship. The young man with the guitar is beautifully placed to make music with the client because our business is about making music with the client. Music will help create conversation and talking points that are welcome distractions from work. In the minutes before the scheduled start of a meeting between two individuals, it's natural to talk about the weather, about the previous day's cricket match, the new James Bond film and so on. All clients are human beings first, with human interests and passions. Natural, unforced conversations about non-business interests and passions help break the ice and become the foundation of a relationship. The more comfortable and close you are to the client, the easier it becomes to talk business, and you move easily into addressing each other by your first names. When a relationship is created, you don't refer to a client by designation, you refer to the client by their name.

Clients are as human as you think you are. They respond, they anticipate, they pre-empt you in the relationship as much as you think you need to do. The TV soap *Mad Men* shows us a lot about the importance of relationships and social interaction between clients and their agency peers. And if you play the guitar you are in a good place, in that you have an interest which is a creative interest that can go beyond the business relationship into a softer, more caring and non-agenda-based relationship. However, don't force-fit the guitar playing into the conversation!

I've come across many people with diverse interests beyond advertising. A partner who retired last year, Brian Featherstone, was head of human resources at Ogilvy Worldwide, and was known as a singer and a guitarist (and often carried his guitar and harmonica, ready to perform if the opportunity arose).

I've never played the guitar, but I'm openly passionate about cricket. It's fairly common in India, where cricket is a religion, and often that the first twenty minutes of many meetings are hijacked by the client and I discussing the performance of the Indian team in the cricket match that India played the day before.

So, what music could be to my guitar-playing friend, cricket is to me and could be something else to someone else. In the past year, in the post-COVID-19 era, no meetings begin without all those present asking about the health and well-being of the others present. That's because, while we have business interests, human interests always remain paramount.

Look at my colleague Kunal Jaswani. He worked at a medium-sized agency first, then went on to work at a very small agency and today is the CEO of Ogilvy India. So, anything is possible. Once you're in, forget your degrees. Thankfully, in most of the larger agencies, it is growth based on meritocracy. You are measured and recognized by your performance and your contribution, and your ability to be a team player. You might be unknown and the small agency that you work for might be unknown but, hopefully, your work and contribution to the agency that you work for is known. Kunal is not an isolated case at Ogilvy; a number of our star performers have come to us from smaller outfits, and their work and contribution was their password to entering Ogilvy.

Look at what is happening in sports in India, especially the post-IPL world of cricket. Of late, the IPL has thrown up a number of exciting young players who have not gone through any 'process'; it was their talent that was impossible to ignore. There's a search process in sports (not just cricket) which is now well-known—professional scouts who travel the country looking for gems. Similarly, we need to learn from sports in business, and create a network of spotters and scouts. Hopefully, more brilliant talent in small towns and small agencies will rise to the surface. It's not as if HR departments are not doing something similar but we do need to disrupt the process for the search for new talent, especially the germ of talent.

Even companies like HUL have had to find ways to address the search for talent beyond the traditional process. HUL, in association with CNBC-TV18, has been running a programme called Lessons in Marketing Excellence (LIME) for a number of years. LIME is an inter-business school case study contest that challenges final-year students to find marketing solutions to live issues. The winners of this challenge get jobs at HUL.

In the first few years, the contest was limited to the best-known B-schools of the country. (The limitation was caused by the format of the contest, which required a joint HUL-CNBC-TV-18 team to visit the campuses taking part.) Post-pandemic, taking advantage of the ability to run the contest digitally and virtually, the contest has been expanded to more educational institutions. This exercise has allowed HUL to find the talent wherever it is, rather than waiting for the talent to find the company.

The Mahindra Group and the Tata Group conduct similar exercises, but my professional involvement with HUL affords me to speak about LIME because of my first-hand experience with the initiative. The advertising industry has attempted, as a collective, something along these lines. Portfolio Night, run by the One Club of Creativity, runs a talent-spotting event across the world. While One Club does a fantastic job, we need to find a way to cast the net wider and catch more young talent from across India.

When you are in a leadership role, you are a kind of role model for many youngsters. That's the time not to take yourself too seriously. Don't sit on a high horse while speaking to a youngster. And not many people will use their power to say anything to a youngster. A very famous creative person who headed an agency used to say jokingly to his newcomers, 'You are working with me, you need to pay me. Why should I pay you? I'm investing in your future.' I don't think it was the right thing to say but I think he handled it well and said it jokingly and still paid them. But to believe that an individual alone is right, and therefore the lord and master of the game and therefore, he can do anything, including throwing money, is not right. You have to be sensitive towards youngsters, to try and understand what the youngsters are seeking.

And this is absolutely no time to be arrogant or to show your power in any way.

When I started doing well at Ogilvy, I was 'noticed' by the industry and made a bit of a name for myself. Not unusually, there were conversations about me in other agencies which were assessing whether I could be approached to get me on board.

Soon, I received a call from a rival agency head. This gentleman, a very well-respected man who was deeply involved in theatre and famous for stunning presentations, accompanied by his creative partner, took me to The Palms at the Oberoi for a coffee. During this conversation, I was praised to the skies. It was apparent that they had studied my career and were aware of the campaigns I had worked on. I was very impressed that they had done so much homework on a young person like myself. After all, sitting in front of me were two of the biggest names in the business of advertising in India. Their praise and the fact that they had spent so much time on me made me feel good, and that's when the theatrics came into play. And killed the game (for me).

The agency head pulled out a blank cheque and said to me, 'Boy, write your fare.'

They thought it was a big display of flair, and I thought it was demeaning. It hurt me, my self-esteem, my pride. I said I was not a taxi; asked to take the cheque; and apologized for wasting their time. And then walked out of The Palms.

When a person walks up and says, 'Piyush Pandey, I want to work with you,' which a lot of youngsters do, I can't respond with 'Do you know who I am?'

If you say, 'Do you know who I am?' or behave in a dismissive manner, you are discounting what the other person *could* be.

Be humble. Be generous. Be sensitive. That's your role as a manager. To get the best out of somebody who has the potential. You're not lord and master. You're the respected citizen of your company, your industry and community. Behave that way.

To me, that meeting was a pivotal learning on how not to deal with youngsters. Over the years, I've obviously learned a lot—too much to count or list. Yet every now and then, I get asked to 'list' what I've learned. So, I wasn't surprised with this question: 'If you had to distil all your learnings into three best learnings, what would they be?'

In a career spanning thirty-nine years, if you ask me to give you the three best learnings it's being a little demanding of me. I have learned from various people: my seniors, my clients, juniors, from the people of India, from my cooks and my aged aunts. I've never stopped learning. I'm still learning. I'm learning a lot from our young partners every day. However, I will attempt to answer this question.

I wouldn't call them the three best 'learnings', I would call them three very important learnings.

And number one and two were both from Mani Aiyer, my first managing director at Ogilvy.

One: Take your work seriously. But don't take yourself too seriously. Those who work with me or have worked with me will testify to the fact that this little teaching made such a huge impact on me that I unconsciously live it every day.

Two: You are not capable of doing *everything*. You might be excellent at something, good at other things and incapable at all things beyond these. So, surround yourself with people who are better than you at various aspects of the game—especially those you are incapable of doing or doing well at. At the end of the day, advertising is a team game. And unless you have a great team, one star player cannot win you a match.

Three: No client is a bad client. It is your responsibility to get the best out of the client to be able to deliver the best for the client.

I would say that these three are really important.

The third learning also connects to the need to believe in strong relationships. To expect someone to trust you from the moment you first meet is an unrealistic expectation. Trust has to be earned. Once trust is earned, liberties follow, and you're allowed to fly.

I've seen clients who were deemed to be 'painful' or 'tough' by my predecessors working on an account or by my competitors who had worked with the client earlier, and I realized that, below the surface, there was a wonderful human being that they were not able to discover. I've had the pleasure and honour of discovering many such lovely people beneath the 'painful' and 'tough' exteriors and many of these discoveries have become my friends ever since.

Some of them have retired. Some of them have moved on to other companies or out of this industry; they may not be my clients but remain my friends.

If you start off on the wrong foot and begin with mistrust, you might miss out on wonderful traits that lie hidden and undiscovered, and you could lose out on a relationship that's good not just for your career, but good for you personally.

# Let me illustrate this for you

The list of people who have become my friends for life is a
long, long one. Let me start my very early days where I dealt
with Muktesh 'Micky' Pant (the young brand manager on a
new brand called Sunlight Detergent Powder when I was a
fledgling account trainee), whom I first met when he was with
Hindustan Unilever. He then went on to PepsiCo and from
there to Reebok India (he was employee number ONE there)
and then to Yum! Foods as CMO.

He's retired now, and I am fortunate to have him as a
friend, even if we haven't done business with each other for
years now.

The story is similar with Harish Manwani, whom I first
met when he was at HUL. Our friendship has prospered as
he moved up the ranks to the level of global chief operating
officer of Unilever, a position he retired from.

An extraordinary friendship is the one with Arun Firodia
of Kinetic; he was one of the first clients I worked with and
with whom we created the 'Chal Meri Luna' campaign. He's
retired now, but still calls me once for a conversation. I call
him once in a while as well, and I believe that I have the liberty
to drop in at his house in Pune announced and unashamedly
expect to be invited to stay for a meal.

I haven't done business with Arun Firodia for decades,
but my gain is the lovely relationship we share.

When you have strong relationships, the trust allows you
to take the client for granted. In these instances, I can do away
with explaining a campaign step-by-step and jump straight to
the creative.

But that doesn't always work. In many instances, you
help the client understand where the journey began, what the
intermediate steps were and how you arrived at the conclusion.

This is important, as you might miss an opportunity if you were too eager to jump straight to the idea. The explanation of the process allows the client to better understand the idea, get comfortable with it and approve of it.

There have been amazing moments when a client I have worked with for a long time gets the idea in a second. There are many clients of mine, including Bharat Puri and Harit Nagpal, who have approved ideas presented on a phone call.

Bharat Puri approved a print ad idea narrated on a call without seeing the visual. The first time he saw the ad was in the newspaper the next morning. He had visualized the ad as described by me on the phone and approved of an unseen ad based on the trust he had in us. I've shared a film idea on the phone with Madhukar Parekh, something that I had thought of over a cup of tea before breakfast.

And after I shared the idea, he approved the film on the phone. There was no script, no mail, nothing in writing and a film had been approved.

Magic like this happens only where there is a long association and a clear understanding on the part of the client that you are a custodian of his or her brand. That you think of the brand before you think of yourself. That you are in the game for a long time and not to win an award just because you had an idea.

Equally, there are client relationships where the depth is not as strong, and where I HAVE to go through a step-by-step, formal process to present an idea.

There is no formula; I try to assess the person we're dealing with.

Some don't have the time or the inclination for the preliminaries—they want just the idea. Others want to understand the rationale and the process, and that's what we give them.

The process starts with the brief. I don't think that a brief is like a ball that a cricketer reads well or badly and plays well or gets out to. A brief is always interactive. You may misread or misinterpret the brief the first time around. But, unlike in cricket, you have a chance to re-read and reinterpret the brief.

And to build on the idea that addresses the brief. The best briefs, to my mind, are bonding agents for the team working on the brief. Somebody has a thought-starter. And then, this thought-starter takes on a life of its own. The team discusses it, adds to it and fine-tunes it.

But there are several chances you get in a relationship to truly understand a brief. I cannot count the number of times I've heard this: 'You didn't get it, Piyush, what I'm trying to say is . . . 'When a client says this, the brief gets sharpened and tightened and the agency team has a much better idea of what the challenge really is.

Similarly, I cannot count the number of times when I've pointed out to a client that a key point that emerged during an iteration was not part of the original brief, and smart clients are quick to acknowledge the lapse.

Never think of a brief as a postcard that you've received; it's ALIVE. Even during pitches for new businesses, you have a couple of interactions. You try your best and understand the brief in the first go during a pitch because in the absence of a relationship, you might have fewer interactions and iterations, and you need to interpret the brief much faster. With an existing client, we have a relationship and have any number of opportunities to arrive at a perfect solution. The strength of the relationship also encourages iterations as both the client and agency look for better and better solutions rather than one that is acceptable.

However, this is impossible in a new business pitch. In this situation, if you don't understand something or have even the slightest doubt about the brief, ask the client immediately, because the client is also seeking a partner who delivers a solution based on adequate information and a thorough understanding of the business challenge. Ask the questions, however stupid they may sound, rather than regret later that you didn't.

# 5

# Not All Who Get the Credit Deserve the Credit, and Why It Happens

How can you get credit for your work?
Do you see conflicts when younger colleagues want to push
through ideas that senior colleagues reject?

It's amazing how many young people have contributed to the creation of many popular ads that I'm mistakenly credited with. There is no ad that I've created on my own; indeed, in many of the campaigns that the media credits me with, my role has been limited. Since I keep repeating that advertising is a team game, my only role in many is that of a player in the team.

Lots of people give me credit for all the work on Fevicol and other brands of Pidilite, Asian Paints and Cadbury's, and many others. In many of the cases, it is definitely not me who is the creator or even the originator of the idea. But often, as a senior resource in the agency, you become the presenter of the idea at client meetings. The creator of the idea could be a young girl or a boy in the office. When we build a team to work on a brand, it is our job, as seniors in the agency, to make the younger or newer team members understand the philosophy of the brands that they are working on. And once you they understand the philosophy and DNA of the brand, the ideas come from anyone in the team, even the junior most. A number of the Fevicol ads that you love are not written by me. Most of the Perfetti ads were not written by me. All the great stuff that has come out on Cadbury's in the last ten years is not written by me; however, it is run through me.

Often, in sports, credit is given to the captain of the team. For example, headlines might say, 'Dhoni's team won'. I think it should always be 'India won'. But since Dhoni is the captain, he gets the 'headline' credit. Similarly, I get the 'headline' credit because I'm a known face to the media and my association with Fevicol is imprinted in the minds of the journalists.

But I have many colleagues who literally do better work that I could on brands, including Fevicol. One day, the 'headline' credit will go to these deserving colleagues.

Seniors need to spend time to explain to team-mates that, whatever the headlines might say, internally all of us know who deserves credit for the campaign. That's another essential part of team building.

There is always a conflict between young minds and seniors, much like you see in a child-and-parent relationship.

For example, as a teen, you want the license to stay out for as late as you want; the parent has the responsibility of ensuring your safety. There is no right answer, and the parent and child negotiate a middle ground. The negotiations go on till the teen earns the confidence of the parent and is given the license to decide on when they will come back home.

The conflict will be there, the conflict should be there. If the conflict is not there, nobody is challenged. The senior is not challenged to recognize a changing world and the young are not reminded of the issues that they need to consider.

It's a balance, which, again, is about mutual respect. As a parent and as a senior in an agency, you move from protector to promoter, to encourager.

Age is not the only deciding factor. Whether you're the older person or the younger person, just because you've got the right to vote at the age of eighteen doesn't mean that from your eighteenth birthday you become wise. It's a natural evolution and an evolution that needs to be respected by both sets.

# What happens when work gets rejected continuously?

If your work gets repeatedly rejected by a client, you have to sit down and worry about the common (client and agency) understanding of the business problem and brief. Repeated rejection is frustrating for all, not just for the agency team. It's for the senior management at the agency and the client to sit down and find a new definition of the brief that both agree on. It's never wrong to realize that something is wrong.

Even the greatest and most successful sportsmen analyse their past games and identify areas that need improvement or significant correction.

If there is a mismatch between what is expected of us and what is presented by us, the work WILL get rejected.

It's more important in the case of an old relationship, where we normally understand each other. In such a relationship, if work is rejected repeatedly, it means that expectations and delivery are not in line and we need to course correct.

# And it does happen with clients old, and new

Cadbury and Ogilvy India worked together for many years to address the challenge of getting young adults, just out of their teens, to consume Cadbury Dairy Milk in a country where chocolate was considered to be only a treat for children.

Children loved chocolates but as they turned into adults, societal norms made it sort of uncool to continue eating them. It was not they no longer liked the taste of the chocolate on

one magic day when they turned adult. Indeed, many young
adults would eat a bar in private when they could not be seen.
However, in India, turning adult cued a sense of responsibility
and frugality, and chocolate, in those days, was seen as an
indulgence and a waste of money.

The Ogilvy-Cadbury team, despite many ideas and
presentations, couldn't arrive at an agreeable solution.

Despite decades of partnership, the pressures of business
forced a multi-agency pitch.

Perhaps the reason that we could not find the breakthrough
idea was that both of us, client and agency, were trapped in
legacy thinking. We decided to explore routes that were free
of the shackles of the past. Both Cadbury and Ogilvy wanted
something new and brilliant, but we needed to let go of the
past 'good' (in the fear that we would lose current market

share). The situation called for radical change in our thinking and the top management at Ogilvy decided to take the big decisions that would enable and encourage brilliance.

And magic happened with 'Kuch khaas hai . . .', which ensured that Ogilvy retained the CDM business.

The rest, as they say, is history. Twenty-eight years later, in 2021, that core idea, through many creative interpretations and campaigns, has been the mainstay of the CDM communication.

What of the pain of the years preceding the magic, the hundreds of iterations and presentations and scripts? Were they all useless? Were they rejections? Not at all; those iterations allowed us to be able to see where the problem lay and demonstrated our commitment to each other.

That was an early learning for me—that rejection is not always rejection but is a starting point for fresh thinking.

# PART TWO

PART TWO

# 6

# Gender Diversity

What about gender diversity?
What is the role of brands and advertising in drawing
attention to LGBTQ issues and the LGBTQ movement?

It's not only age that we need to consider. As times change, there is a clear recognition that society, globally, has been less than fair to women. Thankfully, advertising in India has always welcomed women and deserving women have been promoted regularly, even to the level of CEO.

My first boss at Ogilvy (in 1982) was an accomplished woman, Swati Bhansali. She continued to be my boss for quite some time. At Ogilvy, how can I not mention Roda Mehta who was the first woman to head the media department (when agencies were full-service agencies)? Over the years, many women have headed offices. Hepzibah Pathak has the most complex and profitable portfolio of accounts in her role as vice-chairman of Ogilvy. Kainaz Karmakar is one of our senior most creative directors.

It's not just Ogilvy. Other agencies, too, have not struggled to recognize and reward talented women. Anupriya Acharya heads all the Publicis Groupe businesses in India, Nandini Dias heads Lodestar UM, Swati Bhattacharya heads creative for Draft-FCB in India, Tista Sen is at the top of JWT India, Anusha Shetty heads Grey and so on.

I go back to my first thoughts on qualifications for a job in advertising. Passion for communications. I did not say, 'men with a passion for communications'. Men and women with a passion for communications are welcome. They will grow if they prove their worth and are productive in their jobs.

Much has been made of the lack of safety and of the vulnerability of women in the society that we live in, and that leads to several unwanted questions that are asked of women.

Gender-pointedness is pointless.

# Are you married? When do you plan to get married? Do you have children? When do you plan to have children? Are you confident of travelling?

These are almost gender-pointed questions and we must stop asking them—other than from a view of wanting to help female colleagues based on the answers. We never ask men questions about their marital status, though they get impacted as much as women. A new father will be distracted from work as well; a father could be distracted helping his child with homework or driving his daughter to karate class. Parenthood (which I have not experienced first-hand) affects both parents. The large issue, definitely in India, is concern about the safety of women.

If society makes it less safe for women, it is our job as an organization to eliminate the lack of safety. For example, arranging for transport home after a late evening at work or arranging for a male colleague to see her home without worry.

Thanks to the large number of women in Ogilvy, as an organization, we're more sensitive to the needs of women (in addition to the gender-neutral needs of all employees). We have to be because if we do not create an environment where women colleagues feel safe, we'll find it increasingly difficult to attract talented women. That would be our loss.

If you look at the advertising and communication of the last fifty years, much before CSR was a much used phrase, a lot of brands have been associated with social causes by doing meaningful things and in the process making their people responsible citizens of society rather than just promoting something that was bought. (Genuine) involvement in social causes and social issues generates a lot of goodwill and sends a message that the brand is not only about sales and profits.

Older business houses, like Tata, Birla, Godrej, made investments in areas that they believed needed their support. Hospitals, schools, colleges, clinics, even sports were supported by these companies even when there was no legal requirement to do so.

And while these business houses gave back to society by their investment in societal issues, every product or service brand that carries these names is a beneficiary of the goodwill generated through these activities

These issues and needs change with changing mores in society. Organizations like Mahindra and Pidilite and many more have been doing spartan work in the education of the girl child for decades, feeling that this was a challenge that the government alone could not address. HUL has been at the forefront on the battle to make citizens in rural India aware of the dangers of waterborne diseases, need for personal sanitization and water conservation. In most cases, there is no direct link to a product being marketed by the company and the cause that is supported (and there's nothing wrong if there is) but in all cases, considerable goodwill accrues.

Before I discuss the specific issue of LGBTQ, we need to talk about the challenge of Dalits, Scheduled Castes and Scheduled Tribes in India.

In India, the parallel to the Black Lives Matters movement is the Dalit movement, which never got the media focus and attention that the BLM has received, and the momentum that is required to address a historic wrong.

The caste system prevailing in India has been a handicap to millions of Indians, preventing them from achieving basic needs, let alone their aspirations and ambitions. The government, through reservations in educational institutions and in government jobs has, over decades, done their bit in correcting the wrong, but a lot more needs to be done, especially by the private sector.

Historic wrongs MUST be righted. The treatment meted out to the LGBTQ community is another historic wrong, and the government and NGOs will play their role.

The role of brands and advertising is to shine a spotlight on the issue so that more Indians are aware of the problem, are sensitive to the problem and play their individual role in its redressal.

Whenever there is a group of people who have been wronged by society, there is conflict and there is imbalance, which leads to cracks and divisions in society.

Thankfully, we are beginning to see brands and advertising drawing attention to the LGBTQ challenge; Red Label, through its use of a music band comprising members of the LGBTQ community in a major advertising campaign, kicked off the trend. HUL has followed this up with the positive portrayal of the LGBTQ community in communication for Red Label tea. Tanishq has been portraying the community positively in its ads; even a relatively small player like Bhima Jewellers has entered the fray. The momentum has begun, and I'm confident that it will continue.

As far as the LGBTQ movement is concerned, it's getting attention because we're living in a more 'aware' society. If the LGBTQ movement is supported sincerely by a brand, the brand will be seen as a responsible citizen of society.

As a deeper issue, we must understand the extent of diversity in India and learn to celebrate and leverage this diversity.

We have the Dalits, the Scheduled Castes and Tribes from all corners of the country; to add to the diversity, we have a multiplicity of languages, cultures and habits. We have Jains, vegetarians, vegans and non-vegetarians.

To do truly well in any job, which is a lot more pertinent in advertising, we need to be able to understand and connect with all this diversity.

# Is there something that companies in India and operating within India can learn from the large agency networks?

Teams from agency networks across the country, across the region and across the world meet continuously. The more we meet, the more all of us are exposed to the diversity within our organizations. At the recruitment level, ad agencies try to continuously improve the diversity. There are obvious advantages to internal diversity: if we need a Kolkata-focused campaign, for example, we can quickly put together a team that understands the people, language, cultures, habits and nuances peculiar to Kolkata.

(A lot of agencies do not have this diversity, and it becomes obvious when they communicate in a tone or idiom that is alien to the audience that they are targeting).

In the 1980s, on Mani Aiyer's urging, I created a presentation that was titled 'Beyond Bandra in 17 languages', which I later repurposed into one of my first articles, published in *Brand Equity*.

So, the need for diversity and for understanding more languages and cultures was a conscious call that Ogilvy took in the 1980s—a conscious call made by Mani Aiyer and Suresh Malik. They were clear that we needed to be more than a big-city agency, that we needed diversity. Even in the 1980s, Ogilvy India was a melting pot of different cultures and languages, and was the foundation of the organizational capability to create communication for all corners of India in all languages.

I was one of the symbols of diversity, but we had more. We had people from Chennai and Calcutta who were on the board of the company when I was very young, and that was unusual in advertising.

Gender diversity has never been a problem at Oglivy. In the early years, diversity evolved unconsciously, but of late, there's a conscious approach to the balance.

In the past, even in the 1980s, we had women leaders at Ogilvy—not because they were women but because they were leaders. They happened to be women.

There was Roda Mehta who headed the media, and there were level-one and level-two creative directors across the country. A number of our offices have, over the years, been headed by women.

And today you have Hephzibah Pathak, who has come up the ranks, who's the vice chairman of the company and on the board of our company. She's perhaps one of the most influential and powerful client-facing managers in the country today, overseeing global brands from Mumbai. Our CFO, Hufrish Birdy, is a woman. One of our three chief creative officers, Kainaz Karmakar, is a woman.

All those I speak about have been growing up the ranks at Ogilvy before diversity was a buzzword.

In the prologue or preface or whatever you call it, like we did in the last book about the stories between my father and Ila ji about 'Chidiya' and 'Chai Pakaikya'. My sister just called me up from America, about my father's older brother who wrote a book fifty to sixty years ago, which was called *Chajju ka Chauraha*. Chajju answered all the questions on the chauraha 'in front of all the people who cared to ask'. I am going to refer to this.

# 7

# The Role of Ethics in Advertising or Elsewhere

What about advertising and politics?
Should you take up work for political parties?
In the last couple of decades, there have been many debates
about the role of advertising and the ethics in advertising.
Does advertising manipulate people? Do we influence people
into buying things that they do not require?

There are many more questions addressing this broad area, and I won't list them all.

David Ogilvy probably unwittingly answered all these questions when he said, 'The customer is not a moron. She is your wife.' David said this in the context of the need to tone down what was a loud, hectoring tone in the print ads of those days. I'm attempting to extrapolate David's wonderful line as an answer to questions on the role of advertising and the issue of ethics in advertising.

It is the nature of human beings that, when the occasion demands, we present ourselves in good shape and form. When people attend a wedding, they wear their best clothes. And when people go out to church or the temple or mosque, they go appropriately dressed. They often dress to get noticed at their best—if they want to get noticed.

When brands want to get noticed, they present themselves in their true but best form. The consumer is aware that you're presenting yourself at your best and will buy the brand if she is convinced that it is worth it.

Add to this is the simple truism: You can't fool the consumer twice. Why would a customer return to buy your brand if you did not deliver what you had promised initially? If you are a fly-by-night operator, and not into delivering on your promises, you might get away with it once, and then change your line of business and find someone new to fool once. But if you're in the business to stay, you have to respect the consumer, the consumer's intelligence and the choices available to the consumer. It's your job, as a brand, to present yourself as a meaningful offering to make it to the consumer's consideration set.

That's what advertising does. It allows brands to present themselves at their best and helps brands to make it to the consumer's shortlist out of a sea of choices.

In the context of ethics in advertising, I've received more than a few questions on ad agencies promoting political parties.

In many forums, I've stated that **advertising alone cannot win you elections.**

Elections are won on the ground. Elections are won on beliefs and manifestos. Elections are won on the presentation of the candidates and their ability to connect with voters and convince voters that they would deliver on their promises. The past performance of the candidates is another consideration. How the opposition presents itself is an equally important factor.

It's the same dynamics as, say, two brands of soap targeting a consumer. Which has the better packaging? Which smells better? Which does the consumer trust more?

Advertising provides the air cover. Advertising presents the point of view of the political party in a consumer-friendly fashion. If advertising was the only source influencing the electorate, why would candidates travel thousands of kilometres to hold rallies, go to remote places through poor roads? It's because consumers—the voters, in this case—want that one-to-one interaction with the party, with the candidate, with the leader. So, don't ever think that advertising can win you elections. It is your own success or failure, your own promises, the fulfilment of past promises, your past record, the way you have read the mood of the electorate and created your manifesto to address the needs of the people and how much the electorate trusts your words. That's how elections are won. Elections are not won by advertising slogans.

Advertising does, in politics, what it does in any other situation: It brings the brand into the consumer's consideration set.

That might end up going the other way—is there so little to the role of advertising in the elections? Bringing a party into the consideration set is as complex as bringing a soap or toothpaste into the consideration set.

We craft messages that can be understood efficiently by as many consumers as possible. We try to capture the essence of the party's promise and present this to the voter, making it as attractive to them as possible. And, as with any product, if we find a weakness in the competitor's armoury, we try and take advantage of the weakness.

In a country like India, especially in the parliamentary election, it means that we have to understand the aspirations of people across the country when crafting believable messages. And we have to do that for region after region, in language after language, in medium after medium.

Imagine having to launch a soap or a toothpaste across the country simultaneously to demographically different audiences in a six- to eight-week period.

There's a lot that advertising does.

But, despite all that advertising does, they only claim we can make it that we got the voter to allow a party to enter the consideration set.

# Why did I decide to work on the BJP account? Is there an ethics issue at stake here?

It's apparent that those who asked me these questions are not great fans or supporters of the BJP.

I've never asked anyone, after an election, who they voted for. India is a democracy, and you have the right to vote for the candidate and party of your choice.

I have a right, in any category, to work for the brand of my choice (presuming, of course, that the brand wants to work with me).

In 2014, the news media reported that Prasoon Joshi and I, and our respective agencies would be working on the BJP campaign. Within hours, Arvind Kejriwal, the leader of the Aam Aadmi Party, made a statement to the media asking why people like Piyush Pandey (and Prasoon Joshi) were working with the BJP. (Incidentally, well after this statement was made, before the Delhi assembly elections, AAP approached us to work on the AAP election campaign and we politely declined. We thanked AAP for their interest.)

All political parties enjoy support in the millions in a country like India, but nobody wins an election with a 100 per cent margin. Voters have their choices; people have their philosophies and aspirations and make their choices.

To those who do not support the BJP, my answer is simple: I do like the BJP. And I do support their policies.

(An aside: When we were awarded the BJP account, my colleagues were free to choose not to work on the account if they were uncomfortable with the BJP philosophy, in much the same way that, in earlier times, colleagues have refused to work on tobacco or alcohol accounts.)

That doesn't mean that others are my enemies. I have chosen to support a certain way of thinking. And I would encourage you to support the party best aligned to your set of beliefs. It's exactly like what I said about products. There are many in the marketplace. You may choose Brand X, I may prefer Brand Y. You have your reasons, I have my reasons. The same is true for politics.

In fact, you might be allergic to the soap that I use. And I may be allergic to yours. So, suit yourself. Don't choose something that your skin reacts to. But if it doesn't react on my skin and I get the desired result? Then we both have our own course of action.

Abraham Lincoln famously said, 'You can fool some of the people all of the time, and all of the people some of the time, but you cannot fool all of the people all of the time.'

If a political party wins an election and does not deliver on its promises, it will be rejected when it tries and 'sells' to the electorate the next time.

In a democracy, we get the opportunity to choose our government repeatedly. Think of the soap that you bought. If it doesn't deliver, would you buy the same brand again?

# 8

# Successful Campaigns, Unsuccessful Products

What about advertising for brands that don't deliver?

You remember the dot-com bubble and the way it burst? How vast sums of money were spent on advertising? Many of those entities failed to deliver on their promises and both investors and consumers, in some cases, lost money.

For example, there was much excitement (and an extraordinary amount of media spend) on the launch of HomeTrade. HomeTrade was the darling of the media, helped, of course, by the number of brand ambassadors (all 'celebrities') they signed on, including Sachin Tendulkar, Shah Rukh Khan, Priyanka Chopra and Hrithik Roshan. In a matter of months, the business collapsed and HomeTrade disappeared. More recently, we've seen this with Housing. com (though it is trying to make a revival).

Both of these are great examples of the role of advertising. Good advertising allowed both to be noticed by the consumer in a positive light, but both failed to deliver on the promises made to consumers and other stakeholders. If the consumer believes that the brand ran into bad luck or was not quite perfect, the brand might get a second chance. But if the consumer thinks that the intentions of the brand were questionable, the brand will not be forgiven.

What can we, as an agency, do to prevent such situations? I can only speak for the larger agencies. There is a significant amount of diligence that we invest in before signing on a new brand (and good clients conduct a diligence study on us), starting with a study of the balance sheets, annual reports and income tax returns for the preceding few years in the case of older companies. In the case of new or newish companies, we try and study the backgrounds of all the founders and other key members before agreeing to work with them.

But, in the end, we only create the advertising and not the product. Similarly, we're not responsible for the non-delivery of promises made by a brand.

# 9

# Society, Advertising and Regulation

And what of advertising that upsets sections of society?
Doesn't advertising need to be more sensitive to this issue?

Recently, brands like Imperial Blue (a music CD brand) and Tanishq (a jewellery brand), both brands handled by Ogilvy, were criticized for offending consumers in their communication.

Let's start with our own process at the agency and our own checks and balances. We begin with a simple, non-negotiable rule: We follow the rules of the nation.

Beyond this rule, between the client and us, there are many checks before we even work on a campaign.

We are alive to the sensitivities of society.

We do everything that is needed to ensure that we work with law-abiding companies run by people of repute. Human errors (or differences in the interpretation of the law) may creep in, but the philosophy is to check everything that one can. Often, we sample products and services before signing on a client or working on a new project.

We wait to be convinced that anything sold by a client in India is legal and is approved by relevant authorities.

When we craft communication, we try our best to ensure that the script and storyboard are sensitive to societal norms, and then we are careful that they adhere to the regulations of the Advertising Standards Council of India.

A lot of what we do to ensure that we do not get into needless controversies is 'objective'—background checks, financial checks and so on.

But there are subjective areas which are more difficult to navigate or predict.

Now, coming to specifics. A few people wrote in saying that the 'Men Will Be Men' campaign for Imperial Blue was gender-insensitive. To all of us involved in creating the campaign (or in clearing the campaign), it is a laugh on men and not on women.

If you look at the entire campaign, there are many expressions of the reasons the ads give you to laugh at men. In every commercial it is the male protagonist who is the laughing stock, never the woman. And men think, as they watch the commercials, 'Oh god! This is me! I'm so stupid!'

A few of the 'Men Will Be Men' ads don't even have a woman in the ad, but a woman to make men laugh at themselves is a device that is used.

I have enough feedback to show that women too enjoy the advertising, laughing as they see men as the butt of the joke.

Yet, we see some sections of the media and society projecting this campaign as gender-insensitive. Take a look at the campaign again in the context of what I've written here. As with most brands in a similar situation, we ignore the criticism by suspected vested interests and aggressive trolls.

More recently, Tanishq has been in the eye of the storm thanks to their storyboard of a Hindu-Muslim marriage. Tanishq stands for a woman's control of herself, her life, the way she wants to conduct her life.

Tanishq stands for the woman who wants to pursue a professional career, a widow who wants to remarry, a divorcee who wants to remarry and so on.

All these are in support of the woman who wants control over her own life.

Whenever we come across a current social development that is relevant to the brand, we try and explore a piece of communication.

However, none of this is done for temporary gain; the issue should be significant: it should be an issue that the larger society should support women through, and it should be legally right.

Getting to the recent Tanishq 'Ekatvam' ad, I can talk about specifics, which might make the issue easier to deal with. Let me begin by sharing with you that one of my sisters is married to a Muslim. How many politicians do we know who have chosen to marry across religions? How many movie stars have married across religions? The marriage of people of two different faiths is not a figment of imagination, it's a reality in society. Is it wrong to welcome the partner of a different religion into your house? Does it not happen around you?

If it exists in society, if it is allowed by law, then what is the problem with the communication? There was absolutely nothing wrong with the Tanishq communication either legally or sensitively. Yet Titan (the company that owns brand Tanishq) had to bow down to the pressure caused by a combination of media and unchecked hooliganism, and withdraw the ad. Because I work on Titan, I'm aware that one of the prime motivations for withdrawing the ad was the the threat of physical violence to the Titan showroom staff.

What does the company do in a situation like this? Stand up for what is correct and be responsible for injuries (or worse) that its employees suffer?

It is a very sorry state of affairs that the authorities did not move in to protect a salesman or prevent damage to the retail outlets. I think it would have been a great statement from the ruling parties in the states where these incidents occurred to step in and protect Titan.

Titan broke no laws, the communication met all rules and regulations, there is no law in Indian preventing interfaith marriage, then why didn't Titan get protected? I wonder. I wonder with dismay

While on this subject, I have a question for advertising bodies like the Advertising Agencies Association India (AAAI) or Ad Club or International Advertising Association (IAA) or Advertising Standards Council of India (ASCI): Why did you not take a petition or a plea to the Government of India to protect Titan, to support the communication which was legally and totally in line with the regulations in force? We need our industry to be stronger and able to represent and fight for companies, brands and agencies which find themselves in trouble for no fault of theirs.

If our industry bodies fail to act and political parties continue to ignore such rampant hooliganism, what happened with Titan will happen again and again. The amplification of

the negative sentiment is through irresponsible use of social media and, if ignored and condoned, troublemakers will find their few minutes of fame by doing just what the troublemakers in the Titan episode did.

A deeper debate is required with all stakeholders—the regulators, the industry bodies, the marketing companies and civil society. From my perspective, it's the primary responsibility of the AAAI and Ad Club.

Here's my view: If consumers have an issue with an ad, they are free to explore all legal avenues to stop/ban the ad Complain to ASCI, complain to a ministry, go to the courts of law, file an FIR. What they cannot do is to unilaterally take the law into their own hands and commit criminal acts.

# 10

# Different Clients, Different Strokes

Is it worth working with 'lala' or family-owned businesses?
How different are they from MNC brands?

Unlike with the corporate world, with the owners of family-owned businesses, much of the pre-meeting conversations are almost intimately personal. **We still disparagingly call family-owned businesses 'lala' companies and many in advertising struggle to do business with these companies.**

The problem starts with the use of the term 'lala'. 'Lala' is a term used for a private businessman, particularly those who lack formal education and do not have a background of privilege. Many professionals armed with business management degrees think that they are more evolved than the lala who runs his own company.

Many lalas I have met or worked with are much smarter than graduates from Harvard Business School, but we assume they have conservative mindsets on risk-taking. Many are big risk takers but overlay their risk with the belief that their business is one that will need to last forever—as a legacy that they leave behind for their children and grandchildren to profit from and live off.

It's up to you as a professional to help them understand that advertising works the same way as their businesses did, with investment and patience. They need to understand that it takes time and investment to build a brand. You have to build it slowly, you have to build it surely, you have to build it such that it lasts for generations to come. I refuse to call business, however small, a lala business: it is run by a businessman who runs an organization, feeds families and contributes to the economy and society.

Was Ogilvy & Mather a lala company? Was Bartle Bogle & Hegarty a lala company? Was Leo Burnett a lala company? These were all started by individual businessmen who came together to explore a line of business. The origins of the Unilever that we now know was a small business started by **William Hesketh Lever, first Viscount Leverhulme. Is Unilever a lala company?**

All these companies started off as businesses owned by individuals or a small team of like-minded entrepreneurs. They all started small and local and grew into institutions. Imagine if those who dealt with them wrote them off as lalas.

# 11

# Role of Advertising Agencies

Do advertising agencies create brands?

So often I hear pompous ad agency colleagues claim to have 'created' a brand, which is a rather erroneous perception of the role that agencies play. Brands are created collectively. Agencies only contribute to the creation. I have said many times when someone, with a sense of ownership and with good intention, has said that Ogilvy created the brand Titan, that we did NOT.

Did we create Titan? Did we design the watches? Did we sell the watches? Did we set up the retail network and appoint dealers and distributors? Did we design the supply chain? Did we hire all the people in critical positions at Titan?

No. It was the vision of the management of Titan and the subsequent execution of the vision by the management of Titan. We were part of the execution of the vision, if one could call it that. Titan's vision included the creation of a lasting, enduring brand that would capture the imagination of their target consumers and of advertising that would appeal to all segments of their target audience.

And, as Ogilvy, we were fortunate to be the agency to partner with Titan at the time of the creation of the brand. We were certainly a part of a winning team, and we certainly made some runs to contribute to the victory of the team.

Never take yourself so seriously to the extent that, as the agency working on the brand, you feel you created the brand. Brands are created collectively, not individually.

Did we create Asian Paints? No. Did we create Fevicol? No. But when we got the opportunity to create new brands with these existing clients, were we a partner? Yes.

It's more than a nuance. It's black and white; agencies do not create brands, but we're definitely an important partner in the creation of brands.

Over the years, many people have referred to 'brand' Piyush Pandey. Am I a brand? No. I am not a brand. I am a collection of learning from the people of India, from members of my family, a collection of learning from my clients, a collection of learning from my colleagues, a collection of learning from my juniors.

You call me a brand because you see my face all the time in the media. But am I the creator of Piyush Pandey? No. There are many creators who shaped me, who helped define me and helped me rise to the position that I've been able to.

# 12

# Advertising and Music

The hallmark of Ogilvy India advertising over the years
has been some wonderful music. Where do these influences
come from and what keeps them going?

I come from a state which is very popular for its folk music, and folk music surrounded me as a child. I never learnt music; I can't play any instrument, I can't sing to save my life, but my childhood gave me a slow course in music appreciation. Music surrounded me. One of my sisters is a trained, professional singer. As a result, many folk musicians used to visit our house.

Another sister was involved with the tourism industry, so many of these singers used to drop in at home to explore opportunities for performances. Between the two of them, they created many reasons for singers to visit my house, often resulting in impromptu, live performances. So, music surrounded me completely.

By the time I shifted to Mumbai, my sister Ila was an established singer, performing songs for Bollywood films in addition to her intense involvement with the theatre movement.

I was privileged to meet wonderful musicians and singers, some from the world of Bollywood and others from theatre. A number of classical Indian music maestros were friends of my sister's, and I 'attended' hundreds of informal concerts in Ila's house.

Between the exposure to music in my childhood and the additional exposure during my stay at my sister's house (till I found a place to stay on my own), I all but attended a many-year-long music appreciation course.

Through Ila I met Pandit Hariprasad Chaurasia, Pandit Shivkumar Sharma, Ghazal singer Ghulam Ali Saab, famous Rajasthani 'Maand' singer Allah Jilai Bai and many others.

When I joined Ogilvy, my boss Suresh Malik was a music aficionado, incredibly knowledgeable about all forms of Indian and Western classical music and known to most of the eminent musicians in Mumbai.

I accompanied Suresh to all recordings. Over a period of time, he explained to me his dislike for jingles and for inserting brand names into the jingles.

His mantra was that music should *add* to the script and not repeat the script. Suresh's work underlined the role music plays in our life; it touches your soul and engages your heart.

In advertising, music makes the storyline a lot more engaging.

Thanks to working with Suresh, I met and worked with the great Louiz Banks, P.P. Vaidyanathan, Ashok Patki, Suresh Wadkar, Kavita Krishnamurthy and, in later days, Shankar Mahadevan with Ehsaan and Loy, Dhruv Ghanekar and many more eminent music masters.

In addition, over the years, I have worked closely with my brother, who knows a lot more about music than I do.

Music was very important to Suresh, and as a result, to Ogilvy India. Even if it was a soundtrack in a word-based communication, the role that music played to 'hold' the words together was huge.

We were trained to pay a lot of attention to the music, not think of music as a necessary add on. The music HAD to add to the storyline and could not be dealt with carelessly.

Suresh often used to go and record the music himself with one of the big music directors.

It's a habit I got into early, and a habit that I still practise.

On a number of occasions (including the Cadbury Dairy Milk pitch and the pitch that won us the IPL account) I recorded the music and the song first and added the storyline later.

This was the result of the respect that we accorded to music in the Ogilvy India system, and slowly it became a standard operating procedure.

Most of my younger creative colleagues have also imbibed this ethos; many of our recent campaigns, including all the recent work for 'Dairy Milk Silk', are lifted by the beautiful music.

I must share a story about the now iconic 'You and I' song which was the backbone of the Vodafone (then Hutch) marketing.

Rajiv and (the late) Mahesh, the creative directors on Vodafone who conceived of the film with the pug and boy, planned to buy music to accompany their script.

When I first saw the film along with the client, I told the team, 'Everything about your film is original. Why would you go around buying music? Why don't you record your own? Why don't you write original lyrics?'

I got instant pushback: 'But we are not lyricists.'

I said, 'Nobody is born a lyricist. I was not a lyricist. I wrote a lot of songs. Give it a shot.'

That night Mahesh wrote the lyrics, and the simple, memorable music was created with Rupert, the music director.

Spend a moment thinking about the pug and boy commercial—it's impossible to visualize it without the song playing in your head.

I had learnt these lessons earlier from Suresh Malik. Rajiv and Mahesh learnt the lesson with this experience.

Never treat music lightly. Never be lazy about music. If you can't write something beautiful, get help from someone. Make friends with music directors, have sittings with them. Just rap with them. You'll find the music you need and the magic that your script requires to lift it.

I've been fortunate that when Suresh Malik shot 'Mile sur mein hai tumhara', and 'Desh raag', I got to meet some of the artists I had first met as a youngster; there was Shivkumar Sharma, there was Hari Prasad Chaurasia and other music maestros of that ilk.

Who gets to meet such accomplished maestros in advertising? I did, and many of my younger colleagues have, thanks to the importance attached to music.

Credit for the use of music and for Ogilvy's success in this area must go to Suresh Malik. We all learnt from him. Learnt how to ensure that music was absolutely an intrinsic part of any audio-visual communication we created and create. Even in this digital era, when formats have changed, delivery has changed, Ogilvy's work stands out with the use of music.

So, if it's an audio-visual, never forget the audio. Never be lazy about the audio. That's the legacy of Suresh Malik.

# Stock footage or stock music is a lot cheaper than shooting fresh film or buying the music. How do you convince a client that creating fresh music or shooting is worth the additional budget?

First, it's not true that it's always cheaper; sometimes the RoI on expensive music that has been bought is more than worth it. Ask Sir John Hegarty, who has spent so much time and effort to explore the interplay between music and advertising.

Thankfully, many clients get it and do not need to be convinced. They understand that whether we recommend original music or buying a track, we'll enhance the value. It is never a problem. Over the years, we've commissioned so much music that is memorable and lifts the communication that we can easily demonstrate the value if a client is in doubt.

As with any aspect of cost related to creating an ad, it is up to us to recommend, explain our recommendation and justify any additional cost.

We convince clients to shoot at distant locations, to sign on expensive actors, to commission reputed directors. Why is music any different?

# What is the best investment in music that you have made for your clients or for Ogilvy?

During my career, I cannot remember or count the number of tracks that we created for a pitch or for a presentation which went on to be the final track with no further changes.

How can we assess the RoI on such expenses? We invest in a track and win an account that we handle for years to come.

Over the years, we've used tracks to give the client a better 'feel' of the idea behind the communication. In a majority of cases, it has worked for us.

Suresh never taught us to do 'cheap' music. He taught us to do good music.

And this lesson came to my rescue in 1994, when I wanted music to support an idea I had for Cadbury Dairy Milk for a critical presentation, when we were defending the account.

I discussed the idea with Louiz Banks. He was pressed for time as he was leaving for Kolkata for a performance. We rushed to the studio and recorded the track. The track, presented at a pitch, supported 'Kuch khas hai hum sabhi mein' for more than seven years.

*There's something so real in everyone/*
*there's something so real, ask anyone/*
*it's you/*
*it's real/*
*and the feeling is right/*
*there's something so real in the taste of life*

That's all the lyrics said—it was the music that brought the idea to life.

We've won accounts on the basis of music alone. We were pitching for the Tata Cement account, and I'd worked with Suresh Wadkar to create a memorable track for the campaign idea. We presented to a committee headed by Aditya Kashyap who was the MD of Tata Cement at the time. He heard the music and his face lit up. He stopped the presentation and said, 'This account is yours.' That is the power of music.

Suresh understood the power of music and the role music plays in communication better than anyone else I've met. When we were commissioned to create a film to show national integration (the film depicted leading sports personalities through history), Suresh dispensed with the lyrics, believing that there was no need for them.

The output was a three-minute film showing various sportspersons carrying the Torch of Freedom with music playing in the background. It was brilliant music created by Louiz Banks, with inputs from a hugely involved Suresh. The process involved conversations on the telex machine; 10-foot-long telexes from Suresh to Louiz, explaining exactly what was required. Not surprisingly, the track became a hit across the country.

Every agency needs a Suresh Malik to truly work music into their communication well.

What I could never do, and Suresh could, is to write briefs for the music, saying 'that's where the symphony will come in, that's where the chorus will come in', and so on. Perhaps it's time to learn.

The most important lesson that I received from Suresh was when I was grappling for an idea for a campaign for the National Literacy Mission. As Suresh saw me struggling, he said to me, 'Don't create a song about literacy. Find a parallel.'

As I let my mind wander with this new provocation, I remembered a track that we had created for the Sunlight detergent powder launch conference. This track, which was used only once, was recorded with Kavita Krishnamurthy and Suresh Wadkar.

The song was about the rising of a new sun and of the world coming alive. Thanks to Suresh, I saw a perfect connect with the objectives of the Literacy Mission.

I asked Unilever if we could use this track—a track that they had paid for but would never use again, underlining that it would be used for a public cause. Thankfully, Unilever agreed without a second thought.

What was a one-time investment for Unilever, ran for six to seven years and gave wings to the literacy campaign.

Good music isn't always expensive—one has to be creative. We didn't have to buy music for Suresh and Xerxes Desai's Titan campaign idea because the copyright rules allowed us to use Mozart's Symphony No. 25 (which is the common thread in all Titan ad films) without any royalty payment.

We've been using the same music for over thirty-five years now. We have allowed it to be flexible, changing instruments, changing the beat, making it more contemporary than classical, and so on, but it's always recognizable as the 'Titan' tune.

Suresh first, followed by many creative teams that followed, enjoyed the experimentation with the track (encouraged by Xerxes and the Titan team), and loved the intrigue that it caused. Whenever a new Titan ad was launched, consumers would look up as soon as they heard the first few bars, knowing that it was a Titan ad. But they never knew what the story would reveal.

On a few occasions, we used just a few bars towards the end of the ad. Imagine this: a great symphony created by one of the greatest Western classical composers of the world, being used to market watches to the common citizen of India.

There are many great successes rooted in music. As with Cadbury, we've spent a lot of time on music for all Asian Paints campaigns. Two decades ago, we approached A.R. Rahman to compose the music for the film (through Rajiv Menon, the director of the film). Rahman, then a budding musician, went on to be a winner of an Oscar.

The track Rahman composed was so good that when we had to create a Diwali film in Hindi, I wrote the Hindi lyrics to his track, and it worked beautifully. That's the power of music.

## Piyush, you and your generation in Ogilvy embraced music because of Suresh. Have you passed on to the next generation in Ogilvy the importance of music and how not to dismiss it as just something that you need to add on?

It can't go beyond; it can go past their bosses, but it can't go through me. And they're all very smart people, they've been watching Ogilvy and our work before they joined Ogilvy. So, we don't have to tell them. They've all picked it up. It's visible in the kind of music that has been created for Marico, in the music for Taj Mahal Tea, for Cadbury Silk and so on.

There's no formal process of transference, there's no template teaching. When we're discussing an ad, questions like, 'So what kind of music do you have in mind? Who are you working with?' are normal, so it becomes a part of our DNA.

I think some great music has been created by the team currently in charge. Often, I hear the music only after the campaign is ready.

It's no longer something I spend time thinking about, the baton has passed on.

Music, I think, lives as long—and sometimes longer—than the visual imagery.

I've been asked about the soundtrack of the original IPL film; the questioner remembered it by the soundtrack and not by the visuals.

Go back to what I've written about the IPL pitch; Prasoon Pandey and I combined with the magic of Ram Sampath and the track just blew you away.

It wasn't even a song, it was a recitation of poetry. Overlaid with the music, the poetry became immensely powerful, and that's why it gets into your brain and causes you to remember it after twelve years.

# So, Piyush, what would you say to young people, creative directors especially, on how they can expand their mind music-wise? How should they approach music?

Look hard at the word 'audio-visual'. If you don't think about the audio, you've missed out fifty marks in a 100-mark paper. How much will you score in the other fifty?

Listen to a lot of music. Go to concerts. Youngsters today travel a lot more than we did, thanks to connectivity, affordability and opportunity; go to new places and listen to music.

The other day, my sister, who is a professional singer and was visiting me, was listening to some Nepalese music, because some of my staff members listen to Nepalese music. She found parallels and connections to some Indian folk music.

Why did she stop to sample Nepalese music?

When you hear something that connects to you, lights a spark, stop and listen to it. Record it. It doesn't matter what language the song might be sung in or what instruments are used, try and capture the sound and the music. It'll come in use someday.

Learn from Shankar Mahadevan. He was working on an album. In the course of research for a song or for songs on the album, he travelled to Rajasthan and recorded music with unknown, local musicians because their music inspired him.

If Shankar Mahadevan, a singer-composer of national fame, finds inspiration from unknown musicians, then imagine how much we could learn.

The more we expose ourselves, the more we listen to music, the more we enjoy ourselves, the more we'll want to make magic with music. So, the greater the exposure, the better off you are. Learning music is a continuous process if you're in the business of creativity.

As human beings, it's easy for us to see the benefit of music and see how it connects to us. Why is it so difficult for those in advertising to see the power of music?

Sachin Tendulkar loves music and is a great fan of Lata Mangeshkar. When he's waiting in the dressing room for his turn to bat, he's listening to music.

Music has a soothing, calming impact on your mind. In the days when I played cricket, I used to sing the Beatles number 'Don't let me down' to my bat, unnerving the wicketkeeper.

I have a young staff member at home who is a bit of a free bird. He's a very respectful person, but when he's going about the house doing the vacuuming, unmindful of who is sitting there, he's in his own world singing a Nepalese song.

Neither my wife nor I have ever stopped him because he sings to overcome the tedium of his routine, and the songs seem to make him happy and calm.

Every army regiment has a song that is belted out with pride and sung on long marches or before a battle. The army uses this device to motivate the soldiers.

Music touches us through the day, in all walks of life, in varied situations. It's no surprise then that it works so well in advertising.

## You said learning music is a continuous process. As you grow older, where do you get your exposure to new music, new influences?

First, I actively seek new music, including watching 'India's Got Talent' whenever possible. I'm exposed to old songs being performed and to completely new music.

These days, I'm listening to a lot of stuff that I did not hear as a child because it didn't interest me. I ask Alexa to play, for example, western classical music (music I didn't listen to in my formative years). Whenever I travel to London or New York, I make it a point to see a musical. I've had the amazing opportunity, working on the Hindi versions of Aladdin and Lion King, to put Hindi words to some great tracks sung and written by absolute masters. It was a great exercise, to sit with Prasoon Pandey and sync it to the existing music, giving it an Indian feel.

# 13

# Advertising for Health and Pharma

How different is branding and promotion of the health and wellness industry?

In recent years, many award shows, including Cannes, have introduced specific awards for health. That begs the question if branding and promotion for the health and wellness industry is any different from other industries.

Perhaps the only reason that it's different is the regulation that controls a large part of the business. As awareness of the need to address health is spreading across the world, it is a business that one needs to master and look at very seriously.

There are two broad buckets: ethical products, controlled quite closely by regulations across the world. This is a specialized business, involving a lot more direct marketing to the user/influencer: the doctors, the hospitals, the clinics and so on. While there are regulations, it does not mean that there is no opportunity or need for creativity. There is significant need because with most medicines, categories are overcrowded and there is a need for YOUR product stand out in the clutter. PR is naturally a tool that is widely used for this category.

Other industries with similar challenges include alcohol and tobacco, both of which are regulated. Alcohol and cigarette brands have learned to be creative within these constraints.

The second bucket includes OTC medicines, alternative health solutions, clinics and gyms and salons.

I include gyms and salons because the primary reason for them to exist is because their clients want to be more fit and healthy.

There is little doubt that pharma and wellness communication will boom in the years to come and, at

Ogilvy, we're significantly raising our understanding and ambition in this area.

There are a number of brands that we already handle that are tapping into the newfound awareness of the need to stay safe, healthy and fit. The most visible brand that we handle in India, perhaps, is Savlon from ITC. Savlon, a brand which has changed hands many times, was finally bought by ITC. ITC is investing heavily in the brand, thanks to its philosophy of targeting leadership in any category that it enters. Sameer Sathpathy, CEO of ITC Personal Care, has given us the license to create a significant emotional connect with the consumers, even as we give the consumers adequate rational reasons to buy.

Rather than boring, product-benefit focused communication, we've been able to create ads that get noticed and remembered.

One of the first campaigns that we created was 'Chalksticks', the result of a great partnership between ITC and us.

Diseases like diarrhoea proliferate because of the lack of hygiene, particularly in rural and semi-urban areas and especially with children. We needed to find a way to get children to wash their hands with Savlon before their meals, and that was no easy task. When we realized that in these areas, the old method of children using sticks of chalk on a slate was still prevalent, we saw an opportunity.

ITC developed chalk sticks with Savlon in them. When children washed their chalky hands, they could see the soapiness and smell the disinfectant, a novelty that got them to wash their hands.

ITC distributed these chalk sticks free in certain markets to identified schools, raising the awareness of the need to wash hands as well as raising the awareness of Savlon.

## SAVLON HEALTHY HAND CHALK STICKS

Millions of school kids across India do not use handwash but they do use chalk sticks at school. So what if the chalk sticks were infused with handwash? A simple question that eventually lead to the creation of Savlon Healthy Hands Chalk Sticks. The chalk powder smeared on a kid's palms acted like soap when the hands were washed under water. It was an idea that helped bring about a behavioural change, ironically without the kids having to change their behaviour.

It's not easy to measure the gain to Savlon's brand equity through this exercise, but we're confident that it would be significant.

Savlon operates in a marketplace dominated by Dettol, a brand that almost defines the category. To enter that category and become number one in certain markets is an extraordinary feat by Savlon. This is the beginning of a long battle, and a battle that will be fought with creativity, with great insights, and a 360-degree approach, not just mass media advertising.

As I said earlier, constraints force brands in the health and wellness sector to be more creative in the approach to cut through the clutter, and 'Chalksticks' is an example. (The Chalksticks campaign won the Effectiveness Grand Prix at Cannes in 2018, a fine example of how creativity and effectiveness can go hand in hand in seemingly difficult and boring categories.)

I see no reason why interesting work cannot be done in this area. Those who have read my earlier book would know of Ogilvy's association with the drive to make India polio-free. For decades, this was an effort unsupported by communication; in the early 2000s, it was decided by the administration that the effort needed a push. The Government

of India and UNICEF brought on Amitabh Bachchan as the brand ambassador and, using this asset, we created a bold, aggressive, multi-stage campaign, starting with gentle persuasion to the parents to ensure that their child received polio drops to later shaming those parents who hadn't yet done so. In the final stage of the campaign, we thanked all parents who, by ensuring that their children had taken the drops, played their role in making India polio-free.

If the eradication of polio is not serious business, what is serious business? There is a lot that can be done in the pharma space by regular, good creative minds with an understanding of the category and the challenges in communicating. Many of our colleagues don't want to work on pharma accounts in the belief that the category is boring. How can your health be boring?

Communication has a huge role in fighting against superstition, rigid, non-scientific belief and 'tradition' that comes in the way of helping our fellow humans stay healthy and alive. Look at the challenges that governments across the world are facing with vaccine hesitancy in the context of COVID-19; look at the challenges in getting people to wear masks for their own safety. Communication can, and should, help in such areas.

I see a huge potential in pharma and wellness, and we have the talent to take advantage of the potential. It is a challenge that Ogilvy Worldwide is taking on, and India is going to be an important participant in this ambition.

If we can make cement and adhesives interesting, why can't we make pharma interesting? Why can't we give educate consumers on the benefits of using pharma and wellness products in an entertaining manner rather than in a prosaic, textbook style? Why can't we engage the consumer as we did with Chalksticks?

Look at the boom in traditional remedies. We are a significant and long-standing partner of the Himalaya Drug Company which markets herbal products, cosmetic products and skin products. When we first met them and truly understood their philosophy and their product range, we recognized the opportunity that was ignored by many agencies because the category was seen to be boring.

To give you an idea of the opportunity, Himalaya Drug Company now has over 500 products.

While Himalaya might have been born in 1930, the recent player in the wellness segment is Patanjali, which markets traditional medicines. Patanjali, aided by the visible Baba Ramdev as a promoter, has made deep inroads through extraordinary advertising spends but, to my mind, has failed to create good, incisive advertising.

The challenge we see at Ogilvy is constant. Of course, pharma and wellness are regulated, but the challenge is to create effective and entertaining communication despite the regulations.

Dabur is another company in the traditional cures area that we have been associated with for a long time. In the branded Ayurveda products market, Dabur is the leading name in households across the country. Its core is the creation of high-quality products rooted in Ayurveda and using traditional medicine to address health and addressing hair, dental hygiene and skincare issues.

We've worked on many Dabur brands but let's take the case of Dabur Red, its toothpaste, which we've seen grow into one of the largest players in the market.

One of the challenges with this category is that beyond a handful, most brand owners do not see great value in investing in communication that goes beyond the informational. Recent successes like the Savlon example (and of Dettol, which invests heavily in communication) will help spur interest and add a fillip to the category of pharma and wellness advertising.

Overall, I think we're reaching a tipping point in India in advertising in these areas, and we are set to explode. The ongoing COVID-19 pandemic has heightened the need for sanitization in particular and health awareness and focus in general.

In every category and sub-category that has receive heightened importance and attention as a result of COVID 19, we are going to see a number of brands fighting for leadership and for a greater share of the pie, and advertising will play a significant role.

Today, it is impossible to consume news without hearing the names of every vaccine manufacturer in the world. Currently, globally there is a shortage of vaccines, but that will not be the case as more and more pharma companies develop and get approvals.

In a couple of years, there will be a choice of vaccines available to consumers—which vaccine will be bought?

Today, we see no advertising for the COVID-19 vaccine. In the near future, we will. Because the supply of vaccines will be greater than the demand and, as in most categories, the customer will be king or queen.

That's when the need for advertising will be felt.

We're already seeing a similar curve in sanitizers. In March 2019, as we were made aware of the need for sanitization, the supply could not keep up with the demand; store shelves were empty. Today there is a flood of brands in the marketplace, and the consumer has a choice.

The gap in the market was filled by the 'natural' players like Savlon and Dettol, but also by new entrants such as Asian Paints and Pidilite.

And you could add, literally, a hundred more brands to the list. Some of them would be known brands, others new brands trying to seize the opportunity.

How will all these brands survive in such a hypercompetitive market? It will be branding, it will be product differentiation, it will be market differentiation, and it will be a huge battle for market share.

It's now looking like the beginning of a popular marathon, with hundreds of runners in the frame. The race will continue, and it's only as we reach the home stretch that we will learn which brands have broken away from the pack of laggards, and which brands will win.

Just think of the opportunity and the size of the market in sanitizers alone. If you walk into your local supermarket (or go online) you're staggered by the range of sanitizers—surface sanitizers, handwash, fabric sanitizers, leather sanitizers, sanitizers for your computer equipment, for various parts of the kitchen and so on.

In each of these categories, there are a number of brands. What does the consumer buy?

In addition to the boom in sanitizers, almost every existing—and often unconnected—category is claiming antiviral capabilities, riding on the fear caused by COVID-19. Plywood brands, bedsheets, pillow covers, curtains, duvets, clothing brands all use 'antiviral' as a differentiation.

How many of the brands will last? How many are truly brands? There will be a shake-out; a few will survive and the rest will fall by the wayside.

The survivors will be those who are committed to the category, who are persistent and consistent in their brand-building.

The list of brands that seek to cash in (or to solve real problems, to be fair to some of the players) on the current situation are all the drinks and foods that claim to boost immunity. This would include brands like Horlicks, Bournvita, Complan, Boost and Dabur Chyawanprash. All these players have a new hook—immunity boosting—and will have to create communication that highlights the new hook.

---

### Which is your favourite restaurant?

Sadly, thanks to the ravages of economic change, many of my favourite restaurants, like Vadakombda in Goa, have closed down. Perhaps it's because I've found my comfort food in small, offbeat places rather than in the big, glitzy restaurants.

I do get my comfort food in restaurants like Bukhara or Peshawari at the ITC hotels. All ITC hotels in India serve chicken curry, bhindi, dal and kadak roti, all brilliantly made (in room service, not necessarily in their restaurants).

I choose restaurants that still serve a variety of vegetables. In the recent past, vegetarian menus restrict themselves to aloo and paneer (potato and cottage cheese) in tens of different preparations, squeezing out bhindi, palak, baingan (lady's finger, spinach and brinjal) and so on. When was the last time you had a decent baingan bharta (mashed brinjal) at a restaurant? More to the point, when was the last time you saw it on a menu? Similarly, the dal (lentils) in most restaurants lacks in character, being bland and lifeless. In addition, they don't serve a variety of dals. Being a big lover of dal, my cooks at home, both in Mumbai and Goa, make at least fifteen varieties of dal, the decision of which dal to be served being decided by the rest of the food being made for a particular food.

I avoid restaurants in Mumbai and Goa, the cities I live in, because of precisely this gap.

My favourite line at restaurants is, 'Give me a vegetable dish with the name or names of the vegetables. Don't give me nameless things like vegetable jalfrezi, vegetable korma, etc.'

Forget the cities, this gap exists even on dhabas on the highways now, with the menu dictated by the demand from their consumers rather than by their own legacy capability. It's ridiculous that on a highway between Jaipur and Delhi, Chinese fried rice is available and bhindi is not.

I miss that environment that's gone (replaced by plastic chairs and branding) and the simplicity of the Indian food.

## Why aren't there more Indian-origin global brands?

All of us in communication have been discussing the issue for years: Why aren't more Indian brands becoming global brands?

For a country to have a host of global brands, the first step is in improving the image of the nation-brand.

India needs to have a strong image internationally as a manufacturing nation or as a service industry destination, or as an IT powerhouse and so on, so that brands and companies with ambitions to grow outside India can capitalize on this image.

The last few governments have tried to improve the image, beginning with the Incredible India campaign.

More recently, the India Brand Equity Foundation has been created to 'promote and create international awareness of the Made in India label in markets overseas and to facilitate dissemination of knowledge of Indian products and services'.

That's the role of the government. After that, it's the role of the corporate sector. Do enough Indian companies have the confidence to attempt to go global with their brands?

What is 'global'? Do you have to be present and successful in two or three markets outside India?

Even one significant market outside the home country is good enough and we're seeing a number of examples of success like this.

We're certainly seen as global players in the IT and ITES sector, with players like TCS, Infosys, Wipro, Cognizant and so on succeeding in the mature and large markets of the US and Europe.

But in the past couple of decades, a number of consumer-facing brands have been making inroads internationally.

The low hanging fruit are India's neighbouring countries, including the UAE, where the culture and habits are similar and there is a large presence of Indians and Indian roots in these markets.

So, it's no surprise that Pidilite's products sell well in Bangladesh, Sri Lanka and Nepal; Asian Paints operates in many countries globally, Himalaya and Dabur are making significant forays in international markets. Godrej and Marico do well in the Indian subcontinent as well as in the UAE. Amul has a growing market in many markets that have a large Indian diaspora.

There are many more success stories of smaller Indian brands succeeding abroad, particularly in Southeast Asia and the UAE.

But more promising are the stories like Bajaj, which is a market leader in certain markets in Latin America and Africa or of Mahindra Tractors, which is a significant player in the US and Hero Motocorp, which is making inroads into Mexico, Nigeria, Nicaragua, Kenya and Uganda.

If you look at the history of globalization of brands, it is because either that particular country did not have that category, or a new brand emerged that exploited a clear differentiator.

The first would include companies like Cadbury's, which introduced chocolate to many new territories. The second would include the automotive brands from Japan, which managed to sell cars all over the world because of the considerably lower price.

In the case of a product like chocolate (or noodles), it takes time because it involves habit change, and companies in such situations take a long-term view on the markets they attack.

Mere entry into a new country does not guarantee success forever, because an identified gap might be filled in by not just the newcomer, but also by the incumbents as they fight to protect market share.

Take the case of international banks in India till the late 1990s. They offered the consumer better service, better international transactions and so on. With Indian banks (at the time) failing to get their act together, the international banks in India enjoyed high margins and profitability. All that changed with the emergence of ICICI Bank, HDFC Bank and Axis Bank as they launched as challenger brands to the multinational banks, rather than as challengers to the nationalized banks that existed thus far. They looked, felt and offered services similar to the multinational banks at much lower costs.

But who talks about those old days anymore? Today, we've reached a stage where the multinational banks are in decline, with their market share all but consumed by the likes of HDFC or ICICI or Axis or Bandhan or the nationalized bank, SBI, building on the reach and network, or the most recent entrant, IDFC.

Entering a new market is difficult, and sustaining the battle in a new market is also difficult. Unless brands from a single country are able to make the same credible claim, as Japanese brands across categories proudly touted the 'Made in Japan' story.

And then there are the more complex stories, like the IIT or IIM or the Indian medical colleges story. They've not been built by organizations—they've been built by the success and reputation of a large number of individuals. Silicon Valley, the tech majors, NASA, all are bursting with Indian engineers and MBAs; hospitals across the US and Europe take pride in their India-educated doctors; there are many countries around the world which more than welcome nurses from India. As stories of individuals, including names like Sundar Pichai, Ajay Banga, Indira Nooyi, Satya Nadella, they would hardly be noticed. But look below the surface and a larger, more expressible story emerges. Where did these engineers study? The answer from the majority: IIT and other Indian engineering colleges. Where did these candidates do their course in business management? The answer: the IIMs. And the same would extend to the doctors, nurses and so on.

There are enough Made in India products that excel in the global marketplace; like in the case of Indian engineers in the 1970s, when were too 'individual' to be noticed, Indian brands that are successful abroad are too 'individual' to be noticed.

What we lack is a coherent story that combines the great efforts of all these brands.

Much has been written about Prime Minister Modi's call for us to be 'Vocal for Local'.

To my mind, it is a rallying cry to Indian companies to manufacture high-quality products in India. This serves two purposes: the first is to reduce our import of those products that are currently not being addressed by Indian manufacturers and the second is exporting products that are not currently being exported. 'Made in India' has to go beyond being a great advertising line; it is only when consumers across the world respect these three words that the 'campaign' would be said to have worked.

'Vocal for Local' challenges Indian manufacturers. If we are importing a component for, say, automobiles because the component is not manufactured here, what is stopping us?

In my opinion, it is not a cry to turn nationalistic and boycott goods made outside India or goods made by multinationals in India; it's a call to try and widen our manufacturing base and get our quality up to global standards.

# 14

# Start-up Culture

What do you think about start-ups?
Was Ogilvy India a start-up?

To my mind, 'start-ups' is the most misused term in the current times. Somehow, it seems to mean that only businesses funded by angel investors and VCs and which use technology heavily are start-ups. They don't even have to be new (which I thought would be implicit in referring to a business as a start-up). For example, Zomato was established in 2008—thirteen years ago.

I would define any new business as a start-up, whether it be a kirana shop, cycle-repair shop, Pidilite Industries or an Asian Paints.

At some point of time, they were all start-ups. The difference between today's start-ups and start-ups in a time before the VC funding is that today's start-ups are heavily funded not by the entities that funded businesses in an earlier era, but by angels and VCs.

Funding was available for the good old brick-and-mortar start-ups also. Cooperative banks gave you some money, friends, well-wishers, your family and other relatives lent you what little they could afford, but all that money had to be returned.

But these businesses were funded.

I think there are some fundamental differences between the old era of start-ups and today's crop.

In the old days, entrepreneurs ventured into a new business believing that they would be in the business for life.

- Money borrowed from investors (banks, friends, etc.) had to be returned, mostly with interest
- Some investors owned a part of the company and expected a share of the profits
- The essence of the business was to make a profit, however small, after paying due loans and dividends
- Money to grow the business was available ONLY IF you had a track-record of a well-run, profitable company

Today's start-ups are funded based on a vague idea of future turnover and future profits— with the future often being more than a decade away. So, the focus of the entrepreneur is to design a great dream that can be seen as a great dream by the VC community.

One of the tools that help form that dream is branding and advertising.

Ola existed for years before Uber came to India, but Uber had much more funding, and spent a lot of that funding in building a dream, a story—in advertising, branding and PR.

Much of the money spent today is in anticipation of the battle in the marketplace that will be fought, again, in some hazy date in the future.

That leads us to the other truth of this new culture: when the funders and the founders see dreams differently, the funding stops.

And the company shuts down or is sold (at a huge loss to the funders).

The big difference, then, between earlier entrepreneurs and start-ups in this age is this: one wanted to leave a legacy, the other doesn't care.

Historically, everyone started up somewhere. Today, you would not think of Vodafone as a start-up. But if you go back all the way to 1996, Essar started up and sold to Hutchison Max, which sold to Vodafone.

Think of it. Essar was a start-up.

If you take ITC Foods, every new business beyond tobacco and paper was a start-up. The difference is that, since their roots came from a brick-and-mortar business, these new businesses too were wired, mentally, like all traditional businesses. They had to be profitable, deliver RoI, approach traditional lenders and last forever. Imagine this: ITC's Bingo was a start-up, Yippee was a start-up, the biscuit business was a start-up, their soaps and shampoos were start-ups.

So, starting any new business is, in my understanding, a start-up, and not just today's definition. All of ITC's new business were funded, whether by the parent company, by banks, by other financial institutions and so on. But they were funded based on a projection of profitability in a defined number of years.

All the private banks we hear of today were start-ups not long ago, whether it's ICICI Bank, Axis Bank, Kotak Mahindra, YES, IDFC or Bandhan.

An aside: Bandhan Bank started operations in August 2015. Zomato was launched in 2008.

Which one is referred to as a start-up?

Many of the new age 'start-ups' have failed and died because they were questionable businesses in the first place

Armed with seemingly endless budgets, they crunch the brand-building process by splurging on communication in the media, while ignoring the basic requirements of building a reputation built on believable claims and building a base of satisfied customers.

I'm an investor in White Owl, a start-up which (hopefully) follows the old rules. It has made a good start and I'm hoping that it'll make it into an enduring business.

Ogilvy handles the account of a start-up called Cars24, which has just become a unicorn. For various reasons, I attend most of the meetings that Ogilvy has with them and with Sequoia, the VC. I'm relieved that all these conversations discuss brick-and-mortar metrics like revenue, sales and profits.

Licious is another start-up we worked on and here, too, I'm delighted that the conversations focus on sales, on converting enquiries into business, on the product mix, on the needs of the consumer, on sales and the profitability.

The biggest start-up I was associated with from scratch was the Indian Premier League. It is the most successful start-up which I think of. I saw it from its conception to what we see today.

The IPL was based on the best elements of the English premier league model and the NBA model, tweaked and re-engineered to suit cricket, the ICC and the cricket calendar.

It began as a sharply defined cricket-cum-entertainment offering for the entire family. Minor changes were made based on consumer feedback (for example, the dug-out was added), slowly but surely becoming appointment viewing for the fan.

Communication was used to build the brand and to increase viewership and build loyalty.

The IPL was created as a product that the consumer wanted.

Today it is the number one cricket league in the world, and one of the most profitable sports leagues in the world.

The IPL, never referred to as a start-up, was founded in 2007, only a year before Zomato.

One of the most exciting start-ups that I've seen from day one and been involved in from day one is Titan.

Titan was launched by the Tatas. Tata had an image of being steel makers, automakers, truck makers and so on. Their only foray in a consumer-facing business was with NELCO, the consumer electronic company and Tata Oil Mills, the soap company. These two companies contributed little to Tata's bottom line.

Titan was conceived to launch a modern, consumer focused company competing with the government-owned monopoly legacy brand called HMT and with cheap foreign watch brands.

Xerxes Desai and Tata went about creating that brand with conviction and confidence, bringing on board the latest technology, manufacturing processes, design talent and, of course, great identity and communication.

Today, Titan is equal to watches.

In 1987, when Titan was founded, it was a start-up. A start-up built on a solid foundation and a dream and ambition to build the biggest watch brand in India.

Today, Titan has brand extensions in jewellery, eyewear and personal accessories.

Titan is a start-up story. Talk to anyone who was involved in any form in the heady days of the late 1980s and early 1990s.

And they created a start-up culture, one that enabled them to consider and launch brand extensions. Talk to anyone who was involved in the launches of Titan Eye or Tanishq.

And here's a provocation: our biggest clients have never said that they created Ogilvy. Are they contributors to the creation of brand Ogilvy around the world? Yes, they are contributors. They gave us the opportunity. They participated in it. They were partners in Ogilvy, the brand that I've worked nearly four decades for.

Consider how the brand was built in India.

In the 1970s, Ogilvy (then Ogilvy, Benson and Mather, or OBM) was a loss-making company in India. The then management, headed by Mani Aiyer, got the team to get our act together and focus on winning new businesses. And then, slowly and steadily, we began working with better clients and new brands.

We started small—all companies start small. You begin a new business with all the constraints, especially investment and people, and you have to run your business within these constraints.

Think of Ogilvy, then, as a start-up.

And some of our clients, at that time, were 'start-up' clients.

And since we were a start-up mentally, it was easy for us to understand clients who were themselves starting up. They had limited financial resources and we knew how to deliver to these clients. We delivered more value than they were expecting, building their confidence. As our clients grew, so did Ogilvy.

I cringe every time I hear the reference to 'start-up', because every business was a start-up once.

Take life itself. When a child is just born it can't walk. It first learns to crawl. Then it learns to walk and, as a watching parent, you pace it out. You encourage your child to walk one step and then two. After a week, based on your judgement of the ability, you urge the child to walk five steps and then ten.

Over many years, the child that could not walk when just a baby could become the world's greatest sprinter or the world's greatest marathon runner.

Similarly, no start-up will have the ability to become a category leader and a unicorn on day one. As an agency, you have to help the start-up based on where it currently is and where it next could be, realistically. You have to keep adding value and working together to help the client's business grow.

When ICICI Bank was launched, Axis Bank was launched or, most recently, when Bandhan Bank was launched, we happened to be one of their partners. Did we know that they would be category leaders in the years to come?

They were all start-ups, and we worked with them with the understanding that they were new, young and ambitious. Our contribution, in the early days of all, included their identity, their internal communications, their public relations, and some advertising. In each case, the big-budget TVCs came much later.

Revenues follow our contribution to the building of a brand. As these start-ups grow, our contribution, role and scope of work grow as well. So does the revenue.

The essence of advertising is to help brands grow their businesses; we partner someone small today in the belief that they would be large in the future, and that we will be a part of that growth story.

Bandhan Bank, even before Ogilvy's relationship with it, was a successful microfinance company to begin with, and was subsequently awarded a license by the Reserve Bank of India to launch a scheduled bank. Today, after decades of work, Bandhan is a successful scheduled bank, and we are a part of the journey. We enjoy the journey, we take pride in the fact that we are partners on the journey.

Working with these start-ups is not like assembling a burger in a fast-food restaurant. It's like cooking biryani; it takes time for the dish to be ready. And when it is ready, everyone involved, from the chef to the consumer, is delighted with the result.

# Do promoters need to have a clear vision?

When we speak of start-ups and their founders in a digital world, we often refer to their 'vision' and reams are written about these founders.

I've worked with a number of brilliant start-ups with founders with vision, except that you might not call them start-ups.

These are start-ups with very clear long-term plans, with a will to win and are founded by visionaries with a dream, and you dream along with them.

You work towards actualizing their dream and making the dream a reality.

But it's important that all know that the dream is a dream. We never dream of being 2 per cent richer or more successful than we are today. It's a dream, so we visualize 100 per cent better or 200 per cent better.

Those with vision water down the dream and ensure that the dream is achievable, that it is a target that all involved can work towards achieving.

When P.N. Sharma, one of the managing directors of Ogilvy, and Mani Aiyer started our partnership with Pidilite (in the entity it was then), Pidilite was a small company with a pioneering spirit. They were essentially a B2B business with a great product that made them a small but successful company. The vision of the founder, which was to be number one or number two in any product that they launched, later gave birth to many successful and innovative brands, all of which are leaders.

Pidilite was run by dreamers who dreamt big.

Somebody at Ogilvy saw unusual potential in them. Whether it was Sharma or Aiyer, I'm not sure. But Ogilvy took the decision to partner with Pidilite in its dream and its journey, believing that Pidilite would be a significant player someday in the future and wanting to be part of the success story.

Think about it: in the 1970s, Pidilite would have been considered a 'start-up'. The group's profit in the late 1970s was modest; under Rs 1 crore.

In any sport, when somebody makes a debut, you're investing in that somebody. You believe that he or she is capable of playing at the next level and anticipate the dividends. Ramakant Achrekar the famous coach who coached Sachin Tendulkar in his formative days—saw the potential in Tendulkar and paid disproportionate attention to him. He certainly didn't know that Tendulkar would grow to become one of the greatest cricketers the world would ever know. Achrekar was investing in a start-up.

When you hire new talent in your agency, you are investing in a start-up. You don't know what the person will become three years later. Will they leave you? Will they join somebody else? Will they lose interest in advertising? At the time of hiring, there's only so much you can answer.

But you do think the candidate has the ingredients that encourage you to want to invest in them and you give him the new opportunity.

Like start-ups, every candidate will not succeed; some will fail, some will disappoint, a few will be disasters.

When I was first selected to play for my state in cricket, my captain called me to say that I was playing the next day and added that I would not be dropped for three matches even if I had failed.

The state's cricket managers were investing in me. Many sportsmen have similar experiences and have enjoyed a long rope. And many of them made it because they were given the time to succeed.

So, as an agency, especially when it comes to partnering with a new business, it's a decision you're taking to stand by the 'start-up'. Up to a certain time, give the start-up a chance. Some may grow up to become leading companies of the country. Some may not. Some may become mid-size, and some may fail altogether.

But if you want to reap the benefits of partnering with a start-up, as we did with Pidilite, you need a little belief and you have to earn the trust and confidence of the client.

# 15

# Role of Technology and Social Media

How has advertising changed in the digital world?
What about social media?

Like the history of food, we need to remember all history; everything that has come before us. For example, the mobile phone is a derivative of the original telephone and inspired by the original telephone.

Now, original telephones are seen only in museums.

Museums are a record of the evolution of mankind, whether it be architecture, whether it be art, whether it be science, whether it be technology. Every museum is an inspiration about the roots of mankind, and the wings that can make future generations fly. Purely by inspiration, someone made something or did something that made a radical contribution to a particular field, and museums help us remember the significant changes in our history. The advertising industry must have a museum. Considering the availability and advancement of digital technology, of AR and VR, the advertising museum doesn't need to be a physical one and can be largely virtual. Advertising is a vast practice, practised in the smallest of countries across the world. Studying the history of advertising in all corners of the world will give us a way to learn about the various stages that various societies have gone through as more products and services became available—what consumers wanted, how brands communicated to the citizens, how needs were recognized, how they shifted and how they grew.

A virtual museum could be created at a relatively low cost, and if the major advertising industry bodies came together to create one, it would not be the responsibility of any one entity.

Perhaps a good start would be for each agency to create their own museum. Every agency should have a museum of some kind. Once this happens, if a global committee curated the best from these museums and created a global museum, citizens across the world could see the old and new advertising, understand the context in which the advertising was created, the form in which it was created and the various types of content that existed during various stages of history and the changes in how this content was distributed from time to time. Most importantly, we would be able to understand the impact of advertising on society during various phases of history.

---

### How do you sell a warm blanket in a city like Chennai?

My only chance is to sell it to the ice sellers who sell ice by the kilo on the roadside, who could use the blanket instead of the gunny sack they use to pack the ice because it's a better insulator. I would probably save the cost of the blanket by the reduction in the ice that melts.

If I'm able to prove that the ice melts less wrapped in a blanket than in the gunny sack, maybe I have a business chance.

---

As times change, advertising has changed. So has the way youngsters apply for jobs. As I'm over sixty now, a question from a youngster stumps me. He wants to know how he could deal with the challenge of an algorithm rather than a human being reading his resume when he applies for a job.

This is particularly challenging in a creative business such as advertising. To get out of the clutter, how can you get noticed and convince the powers that be that you are different and can bring more to the game? How can you get your passion and dedication noticed? Wasn't it easier when you could just write out or print out a resume and hand it over to a human being and you were sure that it would be read by a human being?

Even in a completely analogue world, large companies had a process to sift through the hundreds of applications that were received. The first interaction with a company (when you were applying for a job) was an application and a resume.

It's the same today. Even if the resume is being 'read' by a machine (thankfully, we've not reached that stage yet), one needs to make the resume one that would stand out—enough to get you to the next stage, where you will be evaluated by a human being in a first interview.

Make your online resume as interesting and exciting as possible because we are trying our best (certainly at Ogilvy) to ensure that no resume goes unseen.

It's up to you to present yourself in a fashion that we want to meet you and then to interact with you again. We certainly don't want to hire people without meeting them.

But when you send in an application for a job, do you instantly have a human interaction? No. The first step is that a HUMAN being reads the application, so try and make them *read* the application. Write the resume in a style and manner that stands out, differentiates you and gets you noticed. Make the resume exciting, make it a reflection of yourself.

Most importantly, craft it for a human being in the creative business, not for the machine that you thought would read the resume.

Many years ago, Mandira Bedi, now a successful actor, had applied for a job in copywriting at Ogilvy. When her form reached me, it was impossible not to be intrigued enough to meet her. Every question that was asked in the form was answered by Mandira with a limerick. Every single question. When I saw the responses, I said to myself, here's somebody who thinks differently. I met her and immediately asked her when she could join, without a word in the form of an interview.

(It's a different matter that, before she would join, she was offered an amazing break on television for a serial, *Shanti*. She made the most of it and that's how advertising lost Mandira Bedi.)

But the story is not about what she became. The story is about how she made an entry into Ogilvy and was offered a job. We still talk about it. Take inspiration from her story. How do you get noticed? Mandira used the limerick as a device to get noticed. What's your passion? What device do you have that will provoke the reader of your resume to truly want to meet you and have you join their agency?

In the past decade, this must be the most asked question: Why am I not on social media? I get asked this question by my colleagues, by the media, by delegates at conferences, by students at colleges and even by strangers I bump into at smoking lounges.

Let's begin this by saying that, in the early years of social media, I understood very little of it and chose to stay away. As I understood it more and understood it better, I think social media is a great 'invention'. Social media has resulted in a lot of good for us; it has enabled life-changing movements in many countries. It's a great platform for the exchange of thoughts, views, opinions, ideas and, quite simply, news.

But a large part of me feels that social media is also, dangerously, like a razor in the hands of a monkey, and it is misused extensively.

It's a device which is supposed to help us to communicate with the world faster, to reach and interact with people who were otherwise impossible to reach.

It's also a device that enables you to answer immediately. While you are able to answer immediately, it is not a requirement that you answer immediately, and immediate answers have repercussions that cause many problems for users. It's taking away from the simple act of thinking something through before answering a question or reacting to an opinion. It's almost as if one HAS to answer immediately. There are good reactions and there could be bad reactions. On social media, judgements are formed INSTANTLY in reaction to a post of a few hundred characters. (I think social media needs a speed governor as cars do). The power to abuse or harass anyone while you hide behind a cloak of anonymity is more frightening. A difference of opinion with a user causes another user to hate, abuse, tarnish the reputation of the first. The artificial devices of measuring popularity like shares, retweets and number of likes provokes a certain kind of social media behaviour—a behaviour that could be very different from the analogue behaviour of a person.

I'm all for human interaction, but I think the spontaneity needs to be balanced by a bit of reflection and thought. When I talk to people face-to-face, I know the people I am talking to and I know, largely, how they would respond to any statement I might make. As a result, I am able to be both spontaneous and secure.

On social media, I am dealing with millions of people I don't know; anything that I say will be open to thousands of interpretations and can be instantly followed by responses that are angry, abusive or hateful. These responses will trigger reactions in me that can be defensive, angry or hurtful.

I've seen celebrities and industrialists respond on social media instantly and regret the response within minutes as they get bombarded with hate. I can't convince myself that, despite these significant downsides, I need to be on social media.

As time goes on, I understand social media better. I still think that it's a great invention, but I still think it's open to endless misuse. I don't trust myself walking around with a loaded gun in my pocket. Especially when everyone I see is walking around with loaded guns in their pockets.

So I stay away. And till social media becomes a safer place, I will continue to stay away.

# On the issue of fake news, which also is enabled and amplified by social media. What is your reaction?

It's a bigger issue than it ever was, thanks to social media and the ability to amplify fake news. Fake news is largely published by dubious sources and amplified by users sympathetic to particular causes and aligned to the beneficiaries of the fake news. As much as good can be done by amplifying good, much damage can be done by amplifying fake news that seeks to incite violence, sow hatred and divisiveness.

The biggest problem, often, is the anonymity of the source and the anonymity of the amplifiers, with little or no accountability for their actions.

Influencing either like-minded people or gullible people into believing something has happened has resulted in violence, arson, social unrest and even death of individuals. Fake news is a very dangerous weapon; it's like a nuclear material in the wrong hands and can destroy the fabric of a society, a city, a country.

I prefer the analogue version of news: I get my news from brick-and-mortar sources I have faith in.

Social media companies are attempting to address the issue but from what I've seen so far, it's too little. The key culprit is the ability to be anonymous on social media—either as the originator or amplifier of fake news.

When I hear of a news break, I reach out to someone I believe would have a better idea of the situation before I accept the news as the truth.

What is it that stops people from doing a cursory check on any development before amplification? It's the instant reaction that is so dangerous.

# So if you're against instant reaction, why are you on WhatsApp?

I'm on WhatsApp because I know who I am sending messages to and receiving messages from on WhatsApp. There is consent before two people can talk to each other, creating a circle of privacy and trust. On social media, I may make myself known to others, but others have the option of staying anonymous. And I don't like that.

# What do you think the government should do or law should do to prevent anonymity and fake news on social media?

I'm not qualified to make a comment on this. I know that several governments around the world are looking at ways of preventing fake news, ways of knowing the source of fake news. I know certain companies which run social media platforms are considering ways and methods to limit the damage. I hope the world comes to some kind of an agreement on how to deal with this menace.

In life, everyone has to be accountable. As a citizen, I'm accountable to my family, my neighbours, my colleagues, my company. I'm accountable to my city, I'm accountable to my country. And if you have to be accountable, then all around you need to be accountable. That is my biggest concern. Because when there's no accountability, there will be those who take advantage of the situation.

Lots of people use social media to good effect. Governments use it for public service messages. Since the time we've had to live with COVID-19, governments across the world, the UN,

NGOs, pharma companies, healthcare companies and even doctors in their individual capacities have used social media to educate people, to provide all kinds of help, and to save lives of those near and dear to us.

Yes, it's a great platform.

But . . .

You have the bullet train, you have the airlines which take you faster from one place to another. What if there were no safety procedures in place? What if anyone could board, unchecked by security, with guns, with bombs?

Would you still think the bullet train or a commercial flight was safe? Would you still use them despite the obvious advantage of the speed of travel?

## You've stayed far away from technology. In your last book, you mentioned that you don't even operate your e-mail account yourself. Since the pandemic, are you a greater user of technology?

Yes, I am. During the last year or so, I've been forced to. In March 2019, I went to Goa for what was planned to be a short visit to celebrate my wife's birthday, and I've been in Goa since.

And since the wheels of commerce keep moving, the company has had to conduct its business, working within the constraints of these unusual times. I, too, had to learn to work within these new constraints. I had to adopt ways that allowed me to keep in touch with colleagues and clients, and, in the absence of being able to meet physically, the only option was technology.

For a person who has long refused to work on a computer, it hasn't been easy. And the work-from-home limitations and consequent ease of access to my (now) famous assistant Ophelia makes it more difficult.

I have been forced to learn and to learn quickly. Nita, my wife, helped me understand the basics that allow me to communicate. In addition, Vivek, a young member of my household staff who, because of his interest, was sent to attend a computer course, became by daily 'tech support'. In the first few months, I needed Vivek's help to do something as simple as logging on to a Zoom call or other conference calls.

If I'm forced to understand some other tool, Vivek is around. My brother, through a lesson on a phone call, taught me how to light up the room so that I could be seen by other participants.

In a way, I've completed a crash course in the first steps in understanding technology thanks to the pandemic.

By and large, I've got a handle on the technology that I need to be able to conduct my work and I'm comfortable, unless the world and I are required to understand some new tools and I'll have to seek Vivek's help again.

# PART THREE

PART THREE

# 16

# My Boss(es) and Me

How do I work with Andy Main? What is his role in the team and how does that translate to making the team a winning one?

Andy Main is a kind of super-captain, responsible for the overall health and growth of Ogilvy by building partnerships with clients as well as with all Ogilvy's leaders, and I'm one of them, looking after an area of defined and specific expertise. Andy's role is to plan the game. It's not a non playing captain; he also has to play because he brings an expertise that we needed as an agency. Andy, formerly global head of Deloitte Digital and a principal at Deloitte Consulting, brings with him a new focus on digital and the experience of running both digital and consulting practices,

So, he is both a leader and an expert. Other leaders, including me, reporting to him are leaders and experts in our own fields. In this partnership, we respect Andy the captain, and the captain has to build the best possible team to achieve the vision and goals of the company.

The principle remains: we are all part of the team of which Andy is the captain, and the team needs to win.

And you don't win every time; that's the simple truth of sports and of advertising. Or, for that matter, of any business.

In a team game, the first thing that the entire team should believe in is being a good sportsman who enjoys the game, knows how to celebrate a victory and knows how to take a defeat. The same is true of advertising.

To crib after losing a pitch or to fail to win at a recognized and coveted award is bad sportsmanship.

The lost pitch, the missed award is like a game that is over. Learn from the game, improve your game and prepare for the next game after assessing why you lost the previous one. I was fortunate to learn how to deal with both victory and loss when I was in college in St Stephen's. We had a traditional rivalry with another great institution called Hindu College in cricket. On the field, we gave no quarter. But after the match, the tradition was for the entire winning team to walk up to the dressing room of the losing team and say, 'Well played, today was our day. Your day will come.'

That's good sportsmanship. If a competitor wins an award, I never forget to congratulate them personally and cheer for their success.

We were not on the winning side today. But tomorrow is another day.

# 17

# Ageism Is a Lot of Hogwash but Needs to Be Managed

As I grow older, what is my role?
Should I continue to stay in the agency?
Is my contribution worth it?
What is the role of others in the agency who are getting on
in years?
On the flip side, what is the role of the youngest people in
the agency? Is there a conflict caused by ageism?

There is no 'age' in advertising. If there was, I wouldn't have a job.

In the same way that there are no set qualifications to get an advertising job other than a passion for communication, followed by your performance, there is no reason why you should become too 'old' for advertising if the passion is still there and you are able to perform at a good level constantly. As I grow older, my 'performance' includes my ability to encourage and provoke good work by my colleagues.

With youth comes innovation and the spirit to say things in child-like innocence and simplicity. A child often asks questions that stump adults and often leaves the adults wondering why they couldn't have thought of something so simple and brilliant.

The youngsters bring 'knowledge' to the agency, fresh perspectives from their lens, their lifestyles and their age. For example, today it's the youngest in the agency who have the greatest understanding of AR and VR and mobile and social, and of the technologies to come.

The seniors bring with them their understanding of the brand and of communication based on years of experience. Both are required: the youth and the seniors. It's when these two work together as a team that magic happens. It's not easy to spot, but there is a constant change in every agency. The seniors must realize when the youth has something of value to teach them; when something by the youth needs to be recognized and celebrated; when 'wisdom' needs to be imparted and, indeed, when to vacate a space to them and move on.

# What would your career choice have been had you not joined advertising?

To be very honest, I really don't have an answer.

I've always said that I had no clue what job I would do when I finished my postgraduation. My first job, in the tea industry, was due to the fact that my close friend Arun Lal (who was my senior at St Stephen's) had joined the company and forwarded my CV to the management; based on his recommendation, I was hired.

Arun and I had decided, while we were in college, that we would work together, and we did, in my first job. On an evening, provoked by something I said, a friend (Arun Lal, again) remarked that advertising would be a good field for me. I took the advice, applied to a few agencies, got accepted by Ogilvy and here I am.

But after all these years in advertising, I'm grateful to the world of advertising and to the man upstairs. I could begin to imagine an alternative career stream if I was ever unhappy in advertising; in thirty-nine years, I haven't ever been that.

# In forty years, what will people be nostalgic for?

I think nostalgia is always about things that are not available to you. Things that you admire and things that are fading out. A few years ago, a company launched a product called Caravan, an MP3 player superficially designed as a transistor radio and packed with famous and popular old Hindi songs. The product has done well, thanks to the nostalgia evoked by both the songs and the physical form of the product. You get nostalgic about your childhood and your memories of youth, because that's not going to come back. So whether it's after forty years or after 100 years or after 500 years, people will always be nostalgic about their memories of these childhood and teen years. We love to see castles and palaces because of the stories we read as children.

I think people will be nostalgic about food cooked for hours on a slow fire. And there are many chefs in India, like Mr Qureshi from ITC, who used to work with the erstwhile nizams and erstwhile royalty, who has mastered the art of cooking over a slow fire. Some of these wonderful dishes take as long as twelve hours of cooking on a slow.

I enjoy Mr Qureshi's cooking on the rare occasion that I visit his hotel. The tastes, flavours, textures and aromas transport me to a time long gone.

I think people will be nostalgic about the food of an era gone by, specifically 'slow' cooking.

Every once in a while, I'm a guest at a dinner where it is obvious that the food is different; that it's been cooked 'slow'. And the more I think about it, the more I'm convinced that a lot of the future nostalgia will be about food.

Today, we don't seem to have the time to enjoy the art of cooking and all that it entails.

Every old cuisine around the world features wonderful food that is cooked on a slow fire, and with the loss of 'slow' food, we lose a history of something that generations loved. In general, food inspires man; in addition, food inspires creativity. When your stomach is full, all other activities become less stressful.

And the better the food, the better it is.

However mundane it may sound, here's my punt: many years in the future, man will be nostalgic about 'slow' food. I hope by the time we realize this, many young chefs have mastered the ability to cook the recipes that Mr Qureshi brings to life.

While talking about food, I need to answer someone who asked me whether I liked samosas. For the uninitiated, a samosa is 'a triangular savoury pastry fried in ghee or oil, containing spiced vegetables or meat'.

This question is completely out of sync with the other questions that I've received, so my answer might be out of synch as well. The short answer is 'Yes'. I like samosas.

But I love its cousin, the kachori more. Again, for the uninitiated, a kachori is 'a round, flattened ball made of flour filled with a stuffing of baked mixture of yellow moong dal or urad dal (crushed and washed horse beans), besan (crushed and washed gram flour), black pepper, red chili powder, salt and other spices'.

In my opinion, the kachori is best made in my own state of Rajasthan. And it's best made in a small shop called Khuteta Namkeen in Jaipur. (If you ever want the address, email me and I'll share the coordinates.) And since all of you, the readers, are reading his book because of your love for advertising, let me connect the kachori to advertising.

The kachori teaches me that one cannot confine oneself to a template and get noticed. The kachori stays distinct from the samosa in the very shape (the samosa is pyramidical, the kachori is rounded), in the fillings and the spices, and all these differentiate the kachori from the samosa and get the kachori noticed.

One could argue that, essentially, they are the same. Both are batter-fried, both have simple fillings.

But subtle changes make them noticeably different.

Ever thought about why doughnuts have a hole in the middle?

# 18

# Looking Back

What would I change in advertising (if I could)?
Is the role of advertising to create desire?

As times change, as all of us see with these incidents, we need to be aware of the changes around us. And we need to change as well.

**What would I change in advertising** is a question that I'm often asked. To answer it, I need some latitude and broaden the question to '**What would I look to see changing in advertising AND marketing?**'

There's not much that an individual can do; significant change needs the involvement of all the stakeholders.

But today, in our industry, we are beset by an unwanted nuisance: change for the sake of change. The desire to change for the sake of changing is perhaps the biggest curse of both marketing and advertising today, and this is a global phenomenon. When an incumbent team has invested in ideas that are effective in the marketplace, the job of a newcomer is to make it contemporary, relevant and fresh. Your job is not to come in and change it for the sake of changing it. (Always remember that the cost of change is not coming out of your savings bank account but out of the budget of the company and the contribution of shareholders.)

The senior most professionals in advertising, including me, dread the entry of a newcomer in a senior position on the client side. Many of these newcomers immediately call for pitches, even as the existing team of communication partners is doing a good job. They put themselves above the brand; they want to see themselves make a mark, not for the brand to continue to succeed.

Mahak was not pretty enough
for her would be in-laws.
To us, she is beautiful.

She's on the heavier side is all they say
while rejecting countless brides.
We say change your perspective.
Look for beauty, and you'll find beauty.
Look for the flaws and you'll only find flaws.
At Dove, we believe Mahak is beautiful.

To those who make young women
go through this test of beauty,
Dove asks how much beauty is enough?

**Dove**

Look for the beauty. Not the flaws.

Join the movement. Take the pledge.
#StopTheBeautyTest

no digital distortion

Mahak, Delhi

Whether on the client side or on the agency side, a newcomer is not brought in to wreck the existing system but to improve the system and take the brand to newer heights.

Good examples of such continuity are Dove, Nike and Coke. Newcomers on these brands, whether on the client side or the agency side, never drastically change things, but nudge the brand to better places.

On the odd and rare occasion, if the existing system is broken, you might have to start afresh.

But these occasions are both odd and rare.

Let me share with you our experience with Rajasthan Tourism. Significant time and money were invested in a campaign that won the imagination of the consumers, and won awards and critical acclaim. A reverse in the next election saw a change in the 'client', in this case the government

Overnight, the tagline of Rajasthan Tourism changed. There was no study done on whether the advertising worked or not. And nothing else was changed; just the tagline, to one that a previous government had used. You now had a campaign that had a tagline that had nothing to do with the communication that it supported; it was left to hang after a TVC.

How much money was just frittered away because of this change for the sake of change?

I wish I could influence youngsters. I wish I could get senior marketing people to get their brand managers to understand that life is about doing great things to the brand. And great things will happen to you because of that. Don't start with yourself, start with the task at hand. If a player goes out and says, 'Today I'll be the man of the match, no matter what,' how will the team win? Did you win the match? Did you score the runs? Did you take wickets? Did you take beautiful catches? There are people looking at you to take you to the next level of the game. So let your bat do the talking, and not your reputation and your whims and fancies.

Which leads me to another challenge that we see both on the advertising side and the client side. They are convinced that there's a conflict of interest in each other's aims: the first wants to be 'creative' and the second wants to be 'effective'.

Who says that you cannot be creative while meeting the brand's business objectives?

In fact, the purpose of creativity in advertising is to be effective for the brand. Art and business go hand in hand. Lyrics and music go hand in hand. You can express yourself and you can deliver the lyrics in a refreshing fashion. The entire story for most brands I've worked for, and the kind of recognition that people of India have given me, is in the creative expression for brands while meeting brand goals.

That IS the challenge in advertising. And whatever the category, the challenge is to creatively address the brand's business ambitions. Look at the work we've done on Pidilite, Cadbury, Asian Paints, Luna, Pulsar and so on, and you can virtually see the business objectives being met by thoroughly engaging and entertaining communication—a piece of work that you voluntarily want to see again, to talk to friends and family about, and share and amplify on social media.

How do we make our brand stand out? How can you touch people's hearts and minds at the same time? It's not impossible to do, and a lot of competent people across the world do it constantly.

The creative for the launch of Apple Macintosh in 1984 is perhaps the greatest example of touching both the heart and the mind at the same time. In the context of the era when this happened, Apple got consumers involved in what was essentially a boring, low-involvement category.

I've sold toothpaste. I've sold adhesive, chocolate, residential properties, cement, mobile handsets and mobile services, cooking oil, banking, life insurance, non-life insurance, even political parties.

The challenge in each case is the same: how do you create communication that appeals to the heart and to the head?

This gets even more important as we live and operate in a hyper-competitive world where the difference between brands in a category is not as clear as the difference between chalk and cheese.

Brand A might seem to have an advantage here and Brand B might seem to have created a differentiator there. Unless someone comes up with a revolutionary difference, we are in a fairly equally competitive marketplace for the majority of the players. In a situation like this, if you market your brand in an interesting fashion and create an unusual brand image that is based on a truth (that not only appeals to your head but also to your heart), that's a way a brand builds a bond with the consumer and enters the consideration set.

And begins to create desire. (There is a view that creating desire is a 'bad' thing. Desire is not a foreign body injected into a human being's system; it exists within the system but not necessarily on the surface.)

But more important than the creation of desire, which will add your brand to a long list in the consideration set, you need to create clear differentiation.

And in the clutter of me-too products, what is it that a consumer will think of you to select you?

I draw a lot from Apple and the various products that it has created.

Was the iPod the mere creation of desire? On the surface, iPod was added in the consideration set to the hugely successful Walkman.

No, they created something that improved upon the Walkman. So that your choice (in terms of the number of songs that you could 'carry' with you) of music was far beyond the ability of the Walkman.

Did Apple create desire? No. Apple satisfied an existing desire—the desire to carry ALL my favourite music with me wherever I might go.

Apple created a differentiation in a product category that already existed, addressing a known desire. The differentiation was significant enough for Apple to 'own' the category within months of launch.

Addressing desire is relatively easy; creating differentiation is a hard task. But the hard task gives you disproportionately high margins, as all of us have seen with the iPod.

One could argue that Apple saw the desire that others failed to see, and that the iPod addressed the latent, unmet desire.

On the subject of unmet desire, I cannot give you a better example than Burger King's Moldy Whopper. Unknown to most, and unseen by most, is that this 'advertising campaign' was many years in the making.

The 'campaign', if one could call it that, tapped into the unmet desire of the consumer to enjoy food (including a burger) with no preservatives. As we all know, preservatives are inherent to almost all packaged food and fast food. These preservatives add to the taste, presentation, smell and so on. Removing the preservatives overnight would cause the product to completely lose character. As a result, Burger King, over the years, removed preservative after preservative, replacing each with a natural substitute and ensuring that the taste, look and so on were maintained.

The marketing campaign used the device of a burger growing mouldy, only to prove that all ingredients were natural. (The campaign for the Moldy Whopper was created by Ogilvy and the other Ogilvy companies, INGO Sweden [partly owned by Ogilvy] and David Miami [an Ogilvy company] together.)

None of Burger King's competitors could do the same without going through the arduous process undertaken by Burger King.

Burger King saw this latent desire and created a fantastically obvious differentiator. As I think back on this, I wonder: are there more such obvious differentiators in other categories?

At the time of the birth of a category, the role is to create desire for the category.

But, in reality, we don't create desire for the category, in most cases. We create desire for the brand that we work on.

The desire to use a soap exists, but our task is to nudge you to desire a Unilever soap.

Tapping into a desire is not as simple as it sounds because the starting point is to know that the desire exists (as explained above). For example, the fundamental platform for Cadbury's Dairy Milk—Generosity—is based on a deep desire that all of us have to do something nice for somebody else and feel good about ourselves.

The National Literacy Mission 'Each One Teach One' campaign created in the 1990s tapped into the similar belief that people would feel good about themselves when they taught even ONE single illiterate person to read and write. More recently, during the pandemic, we have seen citizens across the world feeling good about themselves as they donated to NGOs or distributed masks, medicines and food to those who needed it.

# 19

# Career Paths

What do you regret about your career?

I don't regret anything about my career in advertising. Nothing significant, that is. If there was something that caused me to seriously regret the act, I wouldn't have stayed in this business for thirty-nine years. I have often had regrets about what I consider minor issues. I might have regretted, say, my brashness in a certain situation or have behaved in an unnecessary harsh way with a colleague in another situation or unnecessarily displayed impatience or dissatisfaction with a colleague on a certain day.

But in any of these situations, I've tried to deal with it by discussing it with the persons involved as soon as possible.

As with any relationship, minor issues do not crop up when you know each other for some length of time; these issues crop up with someone who doesn't know you well. My short tone might be offensive to a colleague who hardly knows me, while it would be ignored by someone who has known me for a few years. When I've upset someone, I've not hesitated to walk across the next morning, and apologized and explained my behaviour or perceived behaviour. I regret incidents. I try and learn from those incidents; I'm not in denial.

What I do regret is not worrying about a brief enough to crack it. Over the years there have been many challenging briefs, and over the years I've figured out how to deal with idea blocks.

When I find something difficult to crack, I shut off for a short while. What could you do? Take a swim, read a book, listen to music, watch a movie. Then come back to the problem. We often read about and discuss 'writer's block' and an idea block is no different. Everyone in a creative field has blocks: a painter, a musician, a photographer, an author and a creative director. You don't always come up with an instant answer in every situation.

Give yourself a break. If you have the confidence and (a bit of) patience, the solution will come to you. In our business, thanks to the pressure that our clients feel, we do not have the luxury of too much patience, but a bit of patience is always helpful in dealing with a block.

Give yourself a few hours, fix yourself a drink, catch up with a friend. That done, come back to the problem and the answer will come.

There are no such things as creative blocks; these are merely speed-breakers that you pass. They're not stop signs on the road. Once in a while, the road to a big idea might be bumpy, but you reach the destination.

Another route to de-blocking that I've used is to chat with those who have no connection with the brief. It could be colleagues who do not work on the account that you're currently dealing with, it could be a family member, it could be a neighbour, and you will be surprised when a stray comment sparks a train of thought that unblocks the block.

There's something beautiful, and productive, about having conversations with varied sets of people who are completely removed from the problem that I'm trying to solve.

Over the years, I've received so many ideas from people unconnected with advertising and marketing from what they said to me about life. Somebody said once to me that, at times, life could become like a balloon which I'm holding in my hand. If I press an inflated balloon at some point, the balloon will bulge elsewhere.

The other way to unblock blocks is to look around yourself, at anything and everything that you can see around you.

When I travel long-distance by road, I look at all the billboards that I pass by and many of them are provocations for good advertising. I read a whole lot of boards when I'm doing long-distance driving. The deeper and more away from urban India one travels, the more intriguing the messages. During a road trip from Jaipur to Delhi, billboards for an eatery called Kings Dhaba, peppered the highway. (I learned that there were many eateries called Kings Dhaba, and each had a different outdoor 'campaign'.)

One Kings Dhaba had the line, 'Tasty, clean and whatever . . .' Three motherhood statements. Another Kings Dhaba said, 'Kings ka khana nahin khaaya toh kya khana khaaya?' (If you haven't eaten food at Kings, have you eaten at all?)

Will these two campaigns win awards? Certainly not. But it gives me an understanding of the kind of language, idiom and insight that works in the market they are located in. And I park the memory of these lines in some corner of my brain, to be retrieved, if required, some other day. Perhaps one day, as I suffer from a mental block on a brief that targets this geography, the memory will come in use.

The highways are rich in inspiration and insight. I shuttle between Mumbai and Goa, often by car (it's a ten-hour drive). The route goes through about 30 kilometres of winding mountain roads. These roads, cut into the green mountainside, are locally called 'ghats', which translates to 'cuts'. The drive through the ghats tests the best of drivers and is a taxing phase of an otherwise easy and relaxed trip, with the driver needing to be continuously alert and cautious.

As you come to the end of the 'ghats', you enter a forested area. At this point, someone—and I have no idea who—has put up a wonderful illustration of a leopard (or maybe it's a wolf; the illustration is not that wonderful) which is jumping with joy in the air and saying, 'The Ghats Are Over.'

The 'ad' captures it all; the relief of the driver as the tough phase of the drive is over. Who created this ad? It's probably been crafted by some official of the Indian Forests Service, responsible for the tract of land we were about to enter. The ad is conceptually great, with the 'illustration' lending great life to the otherwise mundane words—The Ghats Are Over.

My gratitude goes out to whoever creates these gems because they could be my inspiration at a later date when I'm sorely in need of inspiration.

# A good reason to look around you, and to park what you see in the recesses of your brain, is because every little bit helps when you're looking for something new.

And all of us are looking for something new; we're looking to do things better every day. If I'm satisfied with all that I've done in the past, all that I've done till this moment, then life will get very monotonous. I have to search for new excitement, new and fresh ideas.

All of us know how to measure the exposure of the consumer to a certain ad or campaign. Imagine that a campaign has been running for three months. Is the consumer bored with this campaign? If the consumer is bored and tired of the campaign, every time henceforth that they are exposed to the campaign serves to irritate rather than inform and entertain.

Similarly, is the client getting bored with you as you stay the same, with no fresh thoughts and new energy?

I stay motivated because of the need to stay relevant to the brands and clients I work on. Motivation comes because the bar HAS to be raised. If you don't raise the bar or have stopped enjoying yourself, then you might as well retire at thirty-five and say, 'Okay, I have done what I wanted to do.'

But if you're seeking better, then you look for new things or a new way to package and represent the old. How can an old thing excite you? You can go back to the past and put it in a refreshing way. The way people have not seen it. One day,

I'll find use for the ideas that I've seen on highways. They'll be old, but I'll find a way to give them new life.

# The more advertising has existed, the more we have the discussion on what a creative director or team should rely on: rational or gut? The answer is not as difficult as it seems.

If I was doing a painting for myself or for a close friend or family member or if I was writing lyrics for a song to my sister, it's a personal effort and it can be embedded purely in your gut.

But if it's a commercial proposition, if somebody is paying you for it, then the rational should be understood, the gut should be the expression.

If you do not know that you have to reach the peak of Mount Everest, how will you take a new path? You must always know where you need to reach. Always. Once you accept where you need to reach, you might choose not to take the routes taken by the predecessors and take the road less travelled.

As part of my own personal experiments, where I write from my gut, I've written a few pieces of poetry, and I'll share one of these pieces here because it seems appropriate in this context.

I've written something about creating your pathways. I've called it 'Pagdandi'. *Pagdandi*, in Hindi, is a pathway made by people walking on a field or tract of land. *Pag* means feet, and *dandi* is a stick that you wield to brush away the undergrowth. The next traveller finds it easier to use the

ॐ
# पगडण्डी

पगडण्डी भी बड़ी खूबसूरत राह होती है,
इसमें किसी व्यक्ति के पग और हाथ में डण्डी होती है।
डण्डी झाड़ियों को हटाती है, पग घास को दबाते हैं,
और देखते ही देखते रास्ते बन जाते हैं।
पर पगडण्डी और पथ में बहुत फर्क होता है,
पगडण्डी पर कोई नाम नहीं, पथ पर सबके नाम लिखे होते हैं।
अमुक पथ, अमुक पथ, फलाना पथ ढिकाना पथ,
कौन था? कहाँ जा रहा था? क्यूँ जा रहा था? पता नहीं,
क्या सिर्फ सड़क पर चलता था, या इसमें कुछ किया था?
किसी को कहीं ले गया था, या सिर्फ कोने पर डटा था?
पथ पर उसका नाम लिखा जाए, ये किसका नतीजा था?
क्या मिनिस्टर का साला था, या एम.ल.र. का मतीजा था?
वैसे भी पथ मरणोपरान्त होते हैं,
अच्छा है कि इन पथों की आशलाषा भूल जाओ तुम,
जिन्दगी में बेनाम सी कुछ पगडण्डियाँ बनाओ तुम।

pathway that has been created and, over a period of time, as more people use this path, it no longer has to be found; it's there for the world to see. The feet make the footsteps and the stick removes the obstacles and a new path is made—one that didn't exist earlier.

Every mistake that I have made removes an obstacle and makes the path ahead easier to deal with. Let me share some of them.

I've made mistakes, many of them, in my journey as a creative professional.

None of these mistakes causes me to regret it or lose sleep over it.

But the mistakes that I made before I joined advertising—when I pursued a career as a professional cricketer—have caused deep regret and taught me some precious lessons that I've applied in my career in advertising.

I was a very good cricketer in my teens and early twenties. I was good enough to captain the St Stephens team, and subsequently the Delhi University team. Under my captaincy, Delhi University went on to win the All-India Universities championship.

Moving from the university team (as I moved out of the university) I played for the under-22 team for my home state, Rajasthan, captaining the side and contributing significantly as a batsman and wicket-keeper. On the basis of these performances, I was selected to play for the senior professional team of Rajasthan for the Ranji Trophy.

That sounds like a dream run. College team, university team, state under-22 team and then the state team—a journey without a blip or a stretch in waiting.

The Ranji Trophy was where I made the biggest mistake of my life, one that I regret even today. I thought that being selected for the Ranji Trophy team was a destination whereas, in reality, it was merely my entry into the seniors' 'club'. This team required me to perform as well as I had done in the earlier stages for me to make it to the next level, but I failed to grasp what, today, seems to be obvious and evident. I thought that I'd made it to the Ranji Trophy and that I'd be there forever.

Despite a number of chances that my state gave me, I did not deliver the potential that the selectors saw in me and the faith that they reposed in me. Eventually, I gave up and 'retired' before they dropped me.

When I look back at the opportunity that I wasted, I'm appalled. Many of my peers of the time, players I competed with, was a part of the team with, went on to play for India. Some of these names are names you will easily recognize— Kapil Dev, Roger Binny, Dilip Vengsarkar, Arun Lal, Kirti Azad and Sandeep Patil, to name a few. All of these players, my colleagues at the same level at some time during my short career as a cricketer, took their entry into the Ranji Trophy as an opportunity and, unlike me, embraced the opportunity and improved their performance. For them, the Ranji Trophy was the beginning of illustrious careers while for me it was the end.

My terrible fiasco at cricket is something that has affected me deeply and is a lesson learned. Since then, I think hard about 'the end of a journey', and remind myself every day that there's more distance to travel. I remind myself regularly that when a campaign is over, I've got to get ready to do the next one.

I've been part of teams that have won at the most prestigious awards in the world but, the day after the award, I remind my colleagues that we've got to get set for the next one. When we win a new account, I quickly remind myself that this chapter is over; the next one needs to be opened. I never look at a recognition, an award, an account win or accolades as a destination and become contented with it.

As the cricket selectors did, everyone around you—your clients and your colleagues—expects you to go on and do better. They TRUST you to go on an do better. You get promoted not for the achievements of the past but for the potential that is seen in you. Somebody has trusted you with the next response.

My failure at cricket has rankled to the extent that I do not forget it for even a day. The learning from that error helped me grow in advertising for the past thirty-nine years because advertising gave me an opportunity that I refused to blow up the way I blew up my cricket opportunity.

To stay with cricket, I look back at the day I joined Ogilvy as the day I was selected for the junior squad. As I did well, and each time I got promoted, I took fresh guard and decided to try my best to accumulate runs.

If you take that learning and try and retrace my advertising career, I stopped thinking about destinations from the day I joined Ogilvy. I started as a trainee and subsequently got confirmed after the stipulated time as an account executive.

I took a deep breath and tried to understand what the company would expect of me in the years to come; I refused to celebrate the confirmation.

A couple of years later, a few of my peers and I became account supervisors (at a time when an agency like Ogilvy had just a handful of account supervisors).

I took a deep breath and tried to understand what the company would expect of me in the years to come; I refused to celebrate the promotion.

I had more responsibility, and I had to prove my worth at this level.

Somewhere down the line, while I was still an account supervisor, I was drafted into the creative department as copy chief for Indian languages, based significantly on my command over Hindi and my understanding of the people from north India. Being moved from account management to creative was (as it is today) unusual, but the then Ogilvy management, anticipating the need to create communication in Hindi (provoked by the launch of national television in India) laid the foundation for a new capability in the agency.

It was an unusual job. It was probably the first-of-its-kind designation in the industry. What does 'copy chief Indian languages' mean? It meant that Ogilvy was focusing on reaching households that advertising was not reaching earlier. And perhaps the system did not want to upset the existing creative team by designating a servicing person as 'creative'. When I was transferred to this new job, I took it as a huge challenge.

I took a deep breath and tried to understand what the company would expect of me in the years to come; I refused to celebrate this new, odd responsibility.

I had more responsibility, and I had to prove my worth in this role.

The 'copy chief Indian languages' was a short-lived designation, but was a responsibility that formed the foundation of my career in advertising. In a matter of time, I was accepted by the 'creatives' based on my work as copy chief and was promoted to associate creative director, and I became 'mainline'.

On reaching each milestone, I decided to take fresh guard; and told myself that I was starting a new inning and batting on zero.

That has been my approach; I'm always batting on zero and my colleagues expect me to make a big score. That expectation, I think, is why I've been promoted and why Ogilvy still sees fit to have me as a part of the team.

I have never made a career graph. I have never thought of what might happen to my career in the immediate or intermediate future; all I've told myself is that I need to anticipate what the management expects of me and deliver on those expectations.

I had no idea that I would end up as national creative director for Ogilvy or, years later, that I would become chairman of the company in India. I was clueless and pleasantly surprised when, in the beginning of 2019, I was invited by the then CEO of Ogilvy Worldwide, John Seifert, to be his worldwide partner as chief creative officer of the agency. It was not a job I had aspired to or believed I would get.

It came as a responsibility. A responsibility that I've tried my best to do justice to, but it's not a medal on my chest. The Ranji Trophy medal still rattles and makes sounds, which disturbs my sleep from time to time, so I've learned to keep medals far away from me.

Is the job, the designation and the responsibility a pressure? It has never been a burden and never been a pressure. But it's my responsibility not to let my supporters, well-wishers, colleagues and cheerleaders down.

You may let them down by sometimes not delivering the high-quality performance that they expect of you.

But the odd failure or underperformance doesn't end up in your losing support. They forgive the odd incident. But if you are guilty of anything irresponsible, of unacceptable behaviour or an illegal act, that will break hearts and your support will disappear. You will not break their hearts because you did not score 100 in every inning that you play. Even the greatest, Don Bradman, is his last innings, scored a zero and finished with a career average of ninety-nine. So, people forgive you for the odd mediocre performance, but it breaks their hearts when you do something wrong that is unbecoming of a leader they have supported and wanted and encouraged.

With my success, do I crave 'celebrity'? I've never wanted to be one and have no desire to be 'popular'. I'm very happy being Piyush Pandey, blessed with a wonderful wife and family, and a set of close friends. I have the license to walk anywhere, like any common citizen, left to my devices and living undisturbed. I'm very content with my job, my colleagues. I think life has given me much more than I could hope for and dream of.

Have I had embarrassing moments? Of course I have, as all of us have had.

My continuing embarrassment is my inability, at times, to remember the names of people I've met often, and I try and mask the memory lapse with a 'Hi partner' or 'Hi champion', 'Hi hero', 'Hello gorgeous' or whatever.

The single most embarrassing moment was when I was called into a meeting with a client—a new client (whom I'd not met earlier) and his team. The meeting was called for the two teams, in full strength, to meet all the members. As the meeting ended, I handed over my business cards to all the members of the client's team.

And I handed over a card to one of my own colleagues, a colleague I'd never met before.

Another moment of embarrassment caused by this memory failing was at a very close friend's party. I was asked to dance by a friend's fiancée. First of all, I'm a man with two left feet. But it was a friend's fiancée. The music was loud, and I asked her for her name because I had not met her earlier. And she gave me the name, I said, sorry, I couldn't hear, could you tell me again? After having been told her name, I managed to forget it again. Ten minutes later, she asked me, 'Now tell me my name?' And I couldn't.

Each year, like many of the fortunate ones in advertising, I make the pilgrimage to Cannes. And I'm filled with dread as I struggle to remember the names of super-achievers from all corners of the world—many of whom I've met before, perhaps at Cannes the previous year. I go blank, and, often, an accompanying colleague sees my discomfort and puts me out of my misery.

# 20

# The Mystery of My Moustache

Do you wax or mousse comb your moustache?
If it's a wax, which brand is it? If it's a comb,
which local shop?

Many of the questions I received were related to advertising or to business, but there were some questions that lightened the mood, unconnected as they were to work. It was impossible not to anticipate a few about my moustache. Some of these questions were linked to my personality or 'brand', but a few were, well, focused on the cosmetics of the moustache.

Like this one: Do you wax or mousse comb your moustache? If it's a wax, which brand is it? If it's a comb, which local shop?

When nature blessed me with the semblance of a moustache, I had no knowledge of brands, differentiation or desire. There were tens of thousands of men in Rajasthan (where I grew up) with glorious and even 'world-famous' moustaches, so my moustache was different because it was far from glorious.

The truth is, I sport a moustache. The second truth is, I never trim the moustache myself. The third truth is, I never maintain the moustache. And, finally, I never 'train' the moustache.

As a result, I have a healthy, messy moustache for the most part. (An aside: a journalist who saw me at Cannes referred to me in his column as 'the dishevelled creative director from India', pointing to my moustache; this comment was found to be offensive by Shelly Lazarus, the then worldwide CEO of Ogilvy, when she read the column.)

My wife and brother couldn't be bothered about my waxing or 'moussing' my moustache, all they want is for me to get a pair of scissors and trim it often.

I've never 'focused' on the moustache. For example, I don't stare at it when I shave in the morning. But, over a period of time, my moustache became my 'logo'—perhaps because it became a dream for cartoonists and illustrators. I don't know how it became a kind of a logo for me with people.

It was not planned as an idiosyncrasy. As David Ogilvy said, 'If you want an idiosyncrasy, do it early in your life. Otherwise, if you adopt some stupid things later on, you will look stupid.' I had no such plans.

Today, as I look back, I recall only two instances when I've shaved my moustache. The first must have been when I was around fifteen and hardly had a moustache (but badly wanted one). Someone told me that if I shaved it once, it would grow better. And I shaved it off and I got a rocket from my mother, who said, in our family, men whose fathers are alive don't shave their moustaches. As a result, I didn't shave for years after this.

My moustache grew as moustaches grow, and I trimmed it from time to time. And I never thought about waxing or combing it, as most young men don't.

The second time I shaved my moustache was in anger. We were playing a big cricket match at the university level. And the umpire made a mistake and gave me out in the first inning of the game and I was very upset. I went and told my captain Arun Lal, I'm shaving my moustache and I want you allow me to open the innings in the second innings. I shaved my moustache. And then I went in; I was in a rampage. I played incredible shots and scored a lot of runs with vengeance. Thereafter I've never totally shaved my moustache off. Maybe, learning from the cricket experience, I should!

Sometimes it grows a little longer, and somebody complains and my brother cuts a moustache. I've got pictures of that also. I've never taken my moustache too seriously.

Later on, I don't know how it happened, people started gifting me moustache-themed presents. There were t-shirts with a moustache, there were mugs with a moustache, there were ads with a moustache, and the moustache was attached to me more than I was attached to the moustache. So that is the story of my moustache.

It's my brother who's particular that the moustache must not look unruly, especially if I'm going for a big interview, a big ceremony, an award ceremony.

The one time that my moustache helped me was when my wife Nita, on our first evening out, at a bar called Toto's, said, 'Can I hold your moustache?' I didn't know, then, that she would hold my hands for life. And five months after the Toto's incident, we got married. So the moustache is important to me.

Have you ever twirled your famous moustache in a heated or tense make-or-break moment during a client pitch, and followed it with a convincing pitch? I think you've already spoken about this . . .

I never take my moustache seriously, but I take my confidence seriously. I've never had the urge to celebrate with a twirl of the moustache. That is left to India's batsman, Shikhar Dhawan, who enjoys it and gets away with it, with a huge amount of charm. He also doesn't do it to show valour. He does it because that's his style.

Has it helped you in your business? You said David Ogilvy is the man with the red suspenders. You're known as a man with a moustache. What do you think that does in the eyes of people who meet you? Does it help you at all? Perhaps it doesn't win you the pitch; does it help open a door? Does it help open the conversation? What does it do to you?

How can a moustache run a business?

I do not know. There have been bigger people like David Ogilvy who have never had a moustache. It's what you bring to the party that matters. I don't think David Ogilvy won or retained businesses because of the suspenders that he wore. It was his competence that got him the business. While he was known as the man with the red suspenders, I don't think suspenders needed to lift him professionally—they were only intended to lift his trousers.

I think your attire and your looks can't fool anybody. I am also known to my friends and colleagues in the industry as the man with the bush shirt. I only wear bush shirts. Now, is a bush shirt more impressive than a jacket and tie? I don't know. I love wearing a bush shirt and I like seeing my face with a moustache.

We're not in a business where looks matter; it's the work that we do that matters.

It's like asking Unilever, 'Do you sell your products because of your logo?' No, you don't. Nobody sells products because of the logo. The logo becomes a bit of a recognition point. In my case, it was not a planned logo. It stayed with me, and I enjoy sporting it and there's nothing more to it.

To the youngsters who have asked these moustache-focused questions, you should know that nothing about your looks matters, nothing about your fancy suits matters. What matters is how you perform at your area of competence. How you contribute to somebody's business. Always believe in what you bring to the party and not in what you wear. People don't buy things from creative people because they have long hair and wear shorts or ripped jeans. Be yourself.

My work made me known to people—and then they remember me as the man with the moustache. Moustache or no moustache, no one will remember me if it isn't for the work.

## Thankfully, we come to the last moustache-related question to lighten the read. With your grand moustache, which role will you best fit in? Viking Warrior or nineteenth-century Russian field marshal?

First of all, I'm not an actor. Nobody will give me a role for any of these characters. Though, I must say, I did perform a very small, fleeting scene in my friend Shoojit Sircar's film *Madras Cafe*, where it was not the moustache, but my personality that they felt that I could play the role of a cabinet secretary. I don't think that role came to me because of my moustache. It came to me for the totality of my personality, which the director felt could convincingly play the role of a cabinet secretary. I still don't know what the 'personality' of a cabinet secretary is.

# 21

# Life in the Pandemic and Life Beyond the Pandemic

In a post-COVID-19 world, when everything settles down again, do you think you'll be doing less of physical meetings and more of Zoom meetings?

Definitely not. When the world comes back to normal, and I hope that it is sooner rather than later, I would love to meet people regularly, as often as possible.

Nothing gives me greater joy than interacting with human beings in person. Nothing inspires me more than sitting with a group of my colleagues and working towards solving a problem. Nothing inspires me more than hugging a younger colleague who comes up with a good idea in the course of a meeting. Nothing inspires me more than to walk into a branch office and interact with not just my peers, but the members of client teams who might be there.

I have always enjoyed travelling to other offices and meetings with clients, with partners and colleagues I haven't met face-to-face in a while. There's both joy and learning when one attends conferences and seminars across the world. And what these events do is to throw up the chance to meet people, known and unknown, accidentally. This is an interaction that cannot happen on Zoom, and I look forward to such accidents again.

There's nothing greater than human personal interaction. Man is a social animal, and we are designed to meet, speak and interact with each other.

If we remain unable to travel and meet physically, I now know how connect through technology. But will I look forward to moving into that world permanently? Certainly not.

A few months into the pandemic and the first lockdowns across the world, headlines and experts spoke about 'the new normal'. Even as this was being discussed, I rejected the phrase and insisted that there was no such thing as the new normal.

The normal human being is a social animal that believes in contact, that believes in collective work, collective celebration, collectively watching sports, collectively enjoying a movie or other entertainment.

What we are experiencing is not their normal, new or otherwise. The new normal is a combination of the original human being and the new habits and learnings that they've picked up.

We're already witnessing, as these words are being written, the world reverting to the 'old' normal. In countries where vaccination has allowed cities to open up, all the social interaction that we have been missing is back. In the UK, the Euro finals were played at Wembley with a stadium full of spectators. The Wimbledon finals was played in front of a full house. The pubs are packed to the rafters again; restaurants are back in business.

The new normal could be a heightened awareness of the need for hygiene and sanitation. Perhaps some people will avoid very crowded areas.

But for the larger majority, the old is back. The old is the normal.

Closer home, domestic flights in India are full. That is normal. What is not normal is the need to wear masks on board, the need for an RTPCR test to visit certain cities. Not flying is not the new normal.

Thanks to the pandemic, many of us now know a little more about cooking, a little more about cleaning our houses. That's the new normal. The world has seen world wars, it has seen other pandemics. The world has seen worse times when the equilibrium was completely disturbed. Cities were completely destroyed, recreated, mankind reconvened, mankind re-socialized. To go back to the old normal, not a new normal.

While on the subject of the new normal, I completely disagree with the notion, expressed by a number of CEOs, that cost-cutting on travel, hotel stays and physical meetings and all that they entail, will be the new normal.

I think that would be the wrong new normal. If you do not have physical interaction, somewhere down the line business will suffer. Consider the current scenario with me. I still haven't been able to physically meet my new CEO, Andy Main. Andy still hasn't physically met most of the members his core global team. Will he only remain a Dr No from the James Bond film who only appears on the screen and talks to you? Or will you want to meet him physically?

Not meeting physically prevents us from experiencing the chemistry between human beings. All of us would want to know Andy more than we can currently learn from the unidimensional Zoom screen. There's so much we could learn from a meeting at a pub, over a coffee, even over a meeting in a conference room.

Let me give you an analogy. For a moment, forget about work and imagine that you and your mother live in different cities, unable to meet thanks to the pandemic. Now, considering the circumstances, you talk to each other on the phone, on a WhatsApp video call and perhaps even on a Zoom call.

Once things are better, what is the need to go and meet her in person? You could continue with the digital interaction and save on your airfare and other attendant costs. Use the money saved to buy yourself a new iPhone or Bose speakers or expensive bottle of wine.

The same would be true of attending the marriage of a friend or celebrating a landmark birthday or anniversary. Why travel when you could save the money?

None of us would do that because we crave the physical proximity and meeting.

It's the same with necessary business travel. Cancel the travel?

That's complete nonsense.

The new normal may mean reduction of travel and reduction of expenditure, *but it will also mean reduction of human interaction.*

Can companies do away with the need for the travel that allows them to improve their relationships with a critical stakeholder—the dealer, the distributor and, indeed the consumer? Can this interaction be replaced by Zoom calls?

What might happen is that wasted and unnecessary travel will be reduced or cut. But, in well-run companies, there are enough checks and balances to prevent wastage anyway, and it existed in the old normal as well. Was it perfect? No, it wasn't. And I do see many companies improving systems to make the process more efficient.

What will we look for?

Is the travel truly necessary?

Could the length of the trip be shortened?

Will the employee be safe and comfortable despite a shortened trip?

Are the savings justified when measured against the loss of interaction?

We will, as responsible managers, find a healthy balance. It's not going to be either travel or no travel, it will be something in between.

# Will I travel less in a post-COVID-19 world?

Yes, I think it will come down a bit, but that is also influenced by my age. Normally, if I had a meeting in another city at 11 a.m., I would take a flight on the evening before the meeting, so I get to rest and am fresh on the morning of the meeting.

I will maintain my travel pattern, but might make fewer trips than I did earlier, but never cutting travel to what I believe are essential meetings.

In most companies, international travel has always been controlled and completely justified, so there's not much scope for cutting it out. By and large, I know my international travel for the year at the beginning of the year, because my travel would be for scheduled, calendared meetings.

And, to my mind, these meetings are all essential.

In an earlier era was the annual meeting of Ogilvy's creative directors at David Ogilvy's residence in France a waste? Should they have been stopped? How does one measure the RoI for the costs on such meetings?

I speak to clients across India (and a few globally) regularly. Almost every conversation involves the client asking me whether I had returned from Goa, followed by an invitation to catch up on my return to Mumbai or a promise to catch up if they visited Goa.

The need to meet others physically is not felt by me alone; it's almost universal. And while the pandemic has caused us to suspend meetings for a while, they will come back.

# What of Working From Home, and Forced to Stay at Home?

From a health point of view, it was essential for governments across the world to ask citizens to work from home. There is no doubt that the decision to close down factories and offices according to the state of the epidemic was necessary and prudent.

But it hasn't been easy for everyone. The majority of our population does not have the luxury of living in a residence that is conducive to working from home comfortably. A lot of the houses in urban India have aged parents and in-laws living in as well, 'shrinking' the available space.

To compound matters, many houses do not have access to Wi-Fi; others do not have as many devices as might have been needed for school, college and work.

While all wanted to obey the law, being cooped up at home has been particularly difficult on the younger generations. In a city like Mumbai, with many of the younger workforce staying in 'paying guest' accommodations or living in small flats together, the stress is almost palpable, with the youngsters wanting to step out and catch up with friends.

Much has been written about the possible negative impact of young kids being robbed of their ability to meet their classmates, play outdoor sport, even visit the neighbourhood playground. Those who are two and under have spent their entire lives seeing outsiders masked. What will this experience do to them? Will it change their personalities? Will it confine them to limited thinking, thanks to the absence of interaction and experiences other than with the household? There are long-term implications that time will reveal; for the moment, there's enough to worry about.

Will offices shrink? Yes, they will, as the WFH experience has taught all of us that many of our colleagues could continue to work from home even after the lockdown is totally lifted. We are already seeing this trend in countries that seem, now, over the worst of the pandemic.

If we shift dramatically to a WFH era, what will be the impact on the personal lives of people, when office issues and stress combine with work issues and stress? It could be an explosive cocktail that we currently have little knowledge of.

In the creative world, there's another question. What quality work will we do from home when the inputs of a living world are taken away from us? We have technological inputs, but not the feel. The feel of the environment, the feel of people, the warmth of human beings. It's a very difficult time that we are getting into, and it'll take time to find solutions to new problems that will arise.

In the past decade (in India), many companies built creches in their offices, introduced paternity and maternity leave, encouraged employees to exhaust their available leave in order to improve the then existing work-life balance.

Working from home can tilt the balance in the other direction. We will need to find solutions to this. Do we now have to find a 'life-work' balance?

Technology has allowed us to 'read' and interpret each other's verbal language, but what of body language?

Body language reveals a lot and helps us in our social and business interactions. Zoom and other tools do little to help in this area, and it's something that we miss now. What is the impact of the lack of ability to read body language? I don't have the answer other than to say I'm poorer without it.

In a Zoom or other virtual meeting, the ability to converse is defined by the rules of the organizer and unnatural hierarchies have been created. When I go to a college to address students, or when I speak at industry forums, post and pre that event, young people come up to me, and say, 'I want to talk to you about this, I want to talk to you about that.' Often, I gain more from these interactions than the questioners. (That's one of the provocations to write this book.)

We seem to have done a huge number of interactions during the pandemic—perhaps more than we would have done in a similar time-span in a pre-pandemic world. But the experiences are hugely different.

When we attend a webinar, is everyone attending the webinar visible to you while you're talking? Often, there's not even enough time to read the names of the attendees, squeezed as they are in the little boxes created for the purpose. There's rarely enough time to interact with delegates and answer questions beyond those allowed by the moderator or whoever is in charge.

Whatever the advancement of communication platforms like Zoom, there's no freedom of interaction. I've been a beneficiary of such interactions and I'm sure many feel constrained in the absence of the ability.

I feel the absence of interactions most when I'm a member of an award jury sitting at a judging session. A large part of jury sessions is the interaction, the arguments, the debates, the body language, the informal catching up at tea breaks, at lunch and over a relaxed drink in the evening. All these rich experiences are lost to me.

In a world such as the one we live in, the first meeting that I had with David Ogilvy might never have happened.

When I joined Ogilvy in 1982, almost the first thing I did was to read all of David's books. Within months of my joining the agency, David visited India to speak at Ad Asia 1982 in New Delhi. As part of his India visit, he came to Mumbai as well, and even a trainee like me got the opportunity to meet him, chat with him and have a drink with him.

The chat is what has inspired me to stay at Ogilvy for thirty-nine years (perhaps forty by the time this is published).

I'd read his books, seen his 'Magic Lantern' videos and I was already in awe of David. But all of these paled into insignificance when compared to the impact that the physical interaction had on me.

It's the memory of the meeting with Ogilvy that causes me to worry about the absence of physical interaction. Imagine generations of our younger colleagues being denied the opportunity to meet someone they admire and look up to.

## What if that meeting had been virtual?

The pandemic has provoked me to think long and hard about this.

The first constraint: the meeting would have needed an official agenda.

The second constraint: the meeting would have had a defined start time and end time.

When I met David Ogilvy during my career, one on one, there was no agenda. I was free to discuss anything under the sun, however mundane or insignificant or disconnected from the business. Neither of us was looking at the clock to see when the meeting was scheduled to end.

And there were other bonuses, such as my first meeting, when I was a trainee, and David bummed a couple of cigarettes from me.

I will always remember this: David Ogilvy asked me for a cigarette.

I couldn't have given it to him on a Zoom call.

Unless somebody improves on it and finds a new formula, all digital meetings are time-bound. And they are very to the point.

I remember the time when I met the then chief minister of Gujarat (now prime minister of India), Narendra Modi.

The meeting was for us to receive a brief from CM Modi on the five or six key tourism destinations that the state wanted to promote.

The official time allotted for the briefing: twenty minutes.

After fifty-five minutes, he was talking to me about the first destination and was in no hurry to move on to the next one. I don't think that would have happened on a Zoom call—he was talking extempore, passionately and unrestrained.

I can easily imagine what the twenty-minute meeting would have been like. It would have been full of data, squeezed into PowerPoint slides. It would have been cold, clinical and factual.

I would have seen none of the passion, none of the seemingly useless trivia that he shared with us; stories of the coexistence of man and beast in his favourite parts of Gujarat, the changing flora and fauna, the challenges of cattle farmers living on the fringes of forested areas, and how these farmers literally walk alongside the lions from the region.

The face-to-face interaction with CM Modi armed me with insights that, I believe, made the eventual communication richer and more engaging.

This experience answers another question.

# Do I prefer a written brief from a client or do I like chatting with a client on the challenge that needs to be solved?

I clearly prefer the chat—when the client goes beyond cold data and shares the softer, often hidden, elements of the consumer, the product and the business challenge.

# Imagine COVID-19 is behind us and travel is back to normal. Your CEO Andy Main is coming to India. What would you do with Andy Main in India that you cannot do on technology?

What would I do with Andy Main?

Exactly what we had done earlier with Shelly Lazarus, Miles Young and John Seifert.

Well, I'd walk Andy Main around my office and introduce him to all my colleagues personally, right down to the receptionist.

I'd take him to my client's offices and introduce Andy to the team members at each client.

Next, I'd get all my clients and colleagues together for an evening for a drink with Andy, so that the official Andy steps back and the human Andy comes to the fore.

How could Andy do a trip to India and not experience great food at a small, local eatery? Perhaps I'd take him to one, travelling on a Mumbai local at non-peak hours.

In a way, I would try and re-create what David did on his travels to India. He travelled within India by train (many attribute that to his fear of flying), visited every office and went with Mani Aiyer to remote destinations to capture the true flavour of India.

## You've met a lot of celebrities and achievers, including, as you've just mentioned, Narendra Modi. What is the most extraordinary experience you have had with a celebrity?

My most unforgettable experience was the one I had with Amitabh Bachchan.

All of us (in India) have seen his films. And many of you have the desire to meet him in the flesh, to shake his hand, to chat with him. All of us want to know the man better—not just the great movie star.

And that leads me to share an extraordinary experience that I had with him—an experience that is truly impossible in a digital world.

I was shooting with Mr Bachchan in the Gir Forest for Gujarat Tourism. We stopped shooting as the sun set each evening. Every evening, after a short rest and a shower, we would have dinner together. On one of these evenings, after dinner, he said that he was going to Paris the following week to recite his father's poetry to a select audience.

Being the perfectionist that he is, he wanted to practise for the impending performance. 'I want to practise, you sit and listen,' he told me. For the next one and a half hours, Amitabh Bachchan recited the brilliant poetry of Harivansh Rai Bachchan to a captive audience of ONE. ME.

I was privileged to listen to an extraordinary performance, but I also learnt of the respect that Mr Bachchan had for his father's work and the passion that he had for keeping the work alive in the minds of both new and older generations.

These are the softer aspects of life which contribute to creativity, and in a completely digital world, much of this will be lost.

# 22

# Life at Ogilvy

Why have you not left Ogilvy and started your own agency?
What is it about Ogilvy that keeps you there?

This is my thirty-ninth year working at Ogilvy, and I have enjoyed every single day, I have learnt every single day.

I have learnt about the soul of the company that David Ogilvy created. About being connected and concerned about our colleagues, their families, our clients and all stakeholders.

The soul that urges us to hire better than ourselves. The soul that attracts the finest talent and clients to us.

From the day that I joined Ogilvy, I had the opportunity to meet great minds including David Ogilvy himself. As importantly, I've worked with some great colleagues and clients in India, and later in the region and even later across the world.

I've grown thanks to these connections and with the interaction and resultant osmosis. I've learnt from all of them, and I learn every day.

Ogilvy is certainly one of the best agency networks in the world, if you look at the representation across continents. I don't think many other agencies can match that, and that gave me varied experience from people across geographies and disciplines and cultures.

Ogilvy is more than a company, it's a large family. And that's not just my experience. Across the world, there are many of my colleagues who have spent more than twenty, thirty years with Ogilvy. In India, for example, my colleagues Rane, Hepzibah Pathak and Madhukar Sabnavis have been here for at least over two decades.

You will find an Ogilvy alumni association or group in almost any city and country that Ogilvy operates in. These groups are active, vibrant and vocally concerned about developments in the agency they once worked in.

Ogilvy gets into your bloodstream. It certainly got into mine.

With me, it was perhaps more apparent. I stopped getting offers from competitors because they thought it would be a waste of time to even make an approach. I was branded 'un-poachable' as I was 'married' to Ogilvy.

Similarly, I'm often asked why I didn't start an agency of my own, when so many of my peers did. Let me answer the question again.

I've been provoked by the temptation to start the great Indian 'global' agency.

Let me address this.

First, from the day I joined Ogilvy, I 'belonged'. I felt that Ogilvy was MY agency.

For the longest time, I never felt that Ogilvy in India was not an INDIAN agency.

When I travelled abroad for meetings, I always felt that Ogilvy was an INTERNATIONAL agency.

Thanks to the culture created internationally by David Ogilvy and in India by my predecessors Mani Aiyer and Ranjan Kapur, Ogilvy India is truly Indian in our culture, in our expression and in our behaviour, and very international in our tools, our global best practices and knowledge pool.

To add to the above, Ogilvy has more than addressed my aspirations, my needs, my wants and my ambitions. What need would I have to leave Ogilvy and go somewhere else? What is the need for me to start off on my own?

By the early 2000s, Ogilvy was one of the largest agencies in India. If I changed agencies, where would I go? I would never gotten the varied experience and exposure, both Indian and international, in a small outfit. That's good enough reason not to shift, because the experiences and exposure all make me richer as a professional.

On a few occasions, when I've been tempted with the offer of funding for a new agency, the carrot of 'freedom' has been dangled in front of me. I've never been shackled in Ogilvy; I've always had all the freedom that I wanted (it might also be that it's because I don't hanker after unreasonable freedoms; I've always been a respecter of rules and laws). What reasons do people have to start an agency of their own?

Broadly, they do it for three reasons:

1. To make more money than they are making currently
2. They want to see their name on the door
3. They are tired, for some reason, of the agency they are working for.

   I've never had these three problems. I have never opened my promotion letter in front of my boss. I have never been unhappy with my salary and bonuses. I'm more than happy to get to work each morning.

   From the time of my appointment to my meeting with John Seifert in Nashville in early 2019 when he offered me the role of global CCO, I've never discussed money, trusting the company to be fair.

   And I've never been let down.

Let me recount my meeting with John.

He sat me down in Nashville and pulled out a file and said, 'Let me discuss your new package with you.' I refused to look at the open file and told him, 'John, I just want to ask you one question. In your opinion, is it fair compensation for the role?' 'It's fair compensation,' he said.

I asked him to close the file and he did. We didn't speak about the compensation again.

I've been rewarded well for my work and am more than satisfied with the company on this score.

My name on the door? What would I do with it? How would it help me? None of my residences, either in Goa or in Mumbai, has my name on the door. Why would I want a company with my name on the door?

Have I tired of Ogilvy? With each passing year it's easier to answer. While the agency is the same, and many of my clients have been clients of mine for my entire career at Ogilvy, each year brings me new opportunities to do fresh work for long-standing clients.

Why should I get tired of working in Ogilvy when I'm pleasantly bombarded by fresh opportunities continuously?

It's a result of opportunities that Ogilvy gave me that allowed me to work on extraordinary brands and create communication that was well received that saw me honoured at Cannes in 2018 with the Lion of St Mark.

How would I get tired of this agency?

# I've been asked, 'If you started an agency, what kind of people would you hire?'

My response, over the years, has been constant. 'First of all, I don't want to start an agency. Second, I have no idea how I will work without my colleagues who have been the pillars of strength to me.'

Yet, I don't ever forget that Ogilvy is not my inheritance. One day, I will not be here. It's a reality. But I will always be a cheerleader from wherever I am.

A number of my peers—very bright people—took the step to launch an agency of their own.

A few of them started an agency, built it to a certain size and then sold the agency in five to ten years. Their motivation was obviously wealth creation; they had no ambitions or plans to build an institution or a legacy. I have no argument with those who took this route, but it's not something I have felt the urge to do. Some of them have done well, and I am happy for them.

A number of these 'leavers' (and some were from Ogilvy) have disappeared from the big world of advertising in which they were significant players while they were in their earlier agencies or at Ogilvy. I don't hear of many of them.

And it's distressing that some who disappeared—perhaps because their business venture failed—are lost to advertising forever, as a five-to-six-year stint of no work to show makes one irrelevant.

There are some who leave with the clear intent to build an institution. Notable amongst them was Mohammed Khan who established and ran his agency, Enterprise, for more than two decades, selling the agency as he neared the natural age of retirement.

What disturbs me is when someone who has worked at a large agency for a considerable period of time launches his own outfit and immediately badmouths the agency he has left to create a 'story' for the new entity.

I have recently experienced one such example, a colleague from the APAC region.

I wonder why wisdom dawned after decades of being in an agency, doing well at the agency, being rewarded by the agency, gaining fame from the agency and so on.

Doesn't it strike them that such rants are responsible for a significant drop in their own credibility?

# Which is your all-time favourite Hollywood movie and Hindi movie?

There are some movies that I've over and over through the years, so I guess these must be my favourites. I've seen them first in the cinema hall, later on television and now on OTT. On each medium, I've seen them many times.

Judged by this scale (how many times I've seen the movie), my favourite Hollywood movie is a toss-up between *The Godfather* and *The Sound of Music*. The Hindi favourite is *Anand*.

*The Godfather* was a difficult movie to make because the book it was based on was so brilliant. The movie transported me to the New York of the 1940s and 1950s; it transported me to the Sicily of that era, it educated me on the role of the mafia in US society and deep-rooted link of the US to Italy and Sicily. Having read the book, I was amazed by how the movie brought to life not only the main characters, but even the smaller characters like Luca Brasi. Having seen many Hollywood movies by then, the music, with the distinct Italian touch, made me sit up and take notice.

*The Sound of Music*, to me, is the magic of music, the magic of performance and the magic of weaving a story with a war time setting. Julie Andrews and Christopher Plummer captivated me by their performances. But what intrigues me is the way they created a musical that lifted the spirits even though it was set against the backdrop of a very difficult and worrying time—the war.

I've seen a Broadway performance of *The Sound of Music* as well. If I've seen the movie fifty times and still want to watch a Broadway performance, it must be a favourite.

And I think about this: the choice of name. *The Sound of Music*. The name promises nothing else but music; cues nothing else.

The movie is based on a book called *The Story of the Trapp Family Singers* (by Maria Von Trapp).

Imagine if the movie had been called that. A great lesson in branding.

*Anand* is a great story of emotions, of friendships and of a character who is dying but has no fear of death, and features beautiful music.

The production values are understated and simple, not glitzy and shiny as is the case with movies starring big names. The understated production values make the story more authentic and make the characters more real and human.

# 23

# Creativity 2.0

So why are you *still* creating ads?
Do you maintain a creative campaign idea bank for
later use?

Whoever sent me the question hadn't added the stress to 'still', but that is implicit in the question.

I have never thought of myself as someone who created ads, but as someone with ideas that benefit the business of brands.

The majority of these ideas are expressed as ads and, from the days when Doordarshan dominated media, all of us in the business registered as 'ad agencies'.

'Definitely Male', which I just shared with you, was a *business idea* for Bajaj's new creation that we had been briefed on, Pulsar. It was a *design idea* that would inspire the next models. It will find new expression and new uses in the time to come.

It's the media that bottled it and decided that the line is 'an ad'.

Similar is the case with 'Har Ghar Kuch Kehta Hai' for Asian Paints. The line can be—and is—naturally extendable to anything for the house, not just the paint. Thanks to the business that we are in, we approached the brief from the point of view of an advertising agency, not with cracking a business problem with a well-thought out strategy; we will be credited with creating a winning line. If we had been a consultancy, we might have been credited and compensated differently.

How would you influence and change user
behaviour related to owning material things
with which they develop a connection?
For example, a table which has been in the
family from your grandfather's time. How
do you convince the consumer to get rid of
the old and replace with something new?

All old things should not be replaced and many will not be
replaced. There are many factors that propel a replacement:
the end of the utility of the product, new financial ability of
the consumer, a change in the social status of the consumer,
the emotion invested by the consumer in the product and
so on.

If the product is still serving a purpose, if it still delivers
emotional satisfaction, it is most unlikely that it will be
discarded or replaced. Interestingly, the 'Sofa' film that
was created to mark sixty years of Fevicol shows precisely
how a functioning sofa with an emotional value doesn't
get replaced; it changes with the changing times, with the
changing social norms. The story is told through the sofa as
it passes on from generation to generation, a witness to the
increasing prosperity of the family. Only the upholstery keeps
changing; nothing else does. The sofa is witness to the way
the relationship and interactions between husband and wife
has transformed through the decades gone by

The upholstery can be changed as per changing fashion,
changing tastes and the times.

The frame is still strong, and no one saw reason to 'waste'
a good sofa. More importantly, the revamped sofa was not
only functional, it allowed you to live with the memory of

generations gone by and the emotional 'bond' causes the sofa to continue to be loved.

The campaign thought for another Pidilite brand, FeviKwik, is 'Pheko mat, jodo' (Don't discard something that's broken; repair it.)

# How do you find the enthusiasm to work on a product that is essentially boring and low-involvement as Fevicol is? How do keep the team motivated and how do you continue to keep the ideas fresh and engaging?

To declare any product category as boring is to shut your mind to an opportunity.

Before I worked on Fevicol, this is exactly how the creatives in the agency thought—that Fevicol was in a boring category. We had shut our minds and had done nothing to open the client's mind to the possibilities.

Soon after I met the client, I was determined to make Fevicol's advertising interesting. When I expressed this ambition to the client, I found the client was as interested and enthusiastic.

The client believed that there was a clear opportunity to make Fevicol a consumer product in addition to it being a B2B product that led to our suggestion that the communication needed to change and speak in the consumer's language.

The rationale was supported strongly by the management, and the first campaign justified our joint belief in the opportunity.

Since then, we haven't stopped. We've released campaign after successful campaign, unfettered by rules and regulations.

The client gives us complete freedom with our ideas, backs it with comfortable budgets for production and further backs it with adequate media spends.

Except for the Fevicol Sofa ad, which was created to celebrate sixty years of the brand, we've never worked to a deadline on Fevicol (it is the belief of the founder that it is more important to get things right than to meet an artificially created deadline). When we have what we believe is a big 'Fevicol' idea, we meet the client and present the thought. The approval comes instantly.

It would not be an overstatement to say that Fevicol advertising has changed advertising in our country; it's not uncommon to hear entrepreneurs and founders and CEOs say, 'I want to see something like Fevicol.'

And to think that this journey started with what was thought to be a boring brand in a boring category owned by a small company.

The experience of these early years and the response to the first campaigns resulted in an extraordinary relationship of mutual trust between Pidilite and Ogilvy—a relationship that has continued non-stop for four decades.

The success with Fevicol resulted in our involvement with all the products that Pidilite has launched since then, and the first of these brands was Fevikwik.

Fevikwik was much easier to deal with because, thanks to the Fevicol experience, everyone in the agency wanted to work on the brand. When newcomers work on the brand, we take time explaining the soul of the brand so that they don't go off on a tangent with their ideas.

Speaking of which, I did go horribly wrong once.

I was enthusiastic about the need for Fevicol to do more meaningful communication, address deeper issues, and so on. As a result, at the height of the terrorism problems in Kashmir I reworked the 'Dum laga ke haisha' ad.

With India's map as the background, with the focus zooming in on Kashmir as the visual element, the voice-over said, in a very sinister tone, 'Tod do, haisha'. At the end of the communication it said, 'Lagao, lagao, aur jor lagao, yeh Bharat ka mazboot jod hai, tutega nahi.'

We ran it for a few days and then we pulled it off. We said, 'we are about the smile', and this communication wasn't.

The idea might have been a good one but it was, in hindsight, not a 'Fevicol' thought.

There will be other ways in which Fevicol could support the country, there will be other brands whose personality could benefit from 'failed' idea, but it didn't and couldn't work for Fevicol.

At Ogilvy, we spend an inordinate amount of time with our young creative colleagues to get them to understand the Pidilite brands we work on, and I'm constantly amazed by how quickly they understand each brand in the portfolio and how perfectly their ideas fit in with the brand ethos. At the cost of repeating myself (I've said this in many forums, I've said this during interviews), a whole host of my colleagues have worked on Fevicol. Many of the ads are my ideas and many are NOT.

It's amazing how the entire agency understands and loves Pidilite and its brands.

A couple of years ago, when Pidilite launched Roff, an adhesive specifically for tiles, a young colleague, Talha Mohsin, presented a script that stunned me by how perfectly he had captured the Pidilite tone and personality.

It's an idea that had me wondering in admiration, 'Why didn't I think of that?'

The problem was that Roff, as a brand, didn't have the budgets that would do justice to Talha's idea. Refusing to be defeated, Talha took the script across to Prasoon Pandey who loved the thought.

Prasoon managed to shoot this film at an affordable cost by combining this shoot with another that was scheduled, and thus considerably cutting logistics and shoot infrastructure costs.

The result? A marvellous film and a worthy addition to the Pidilite portfolio of great advertising.

## Do you maintain a creative campaign idea bank for later use?

I definitely don't throw away an idea. Never. In fact, my brother Prasoon Pandey actually has a box in which he keeps ideas that he can access whenever he wants to, ideas that he believes will be useful to him in the future.

In my own case, in 1997–98, we had pitched for an air-conditioner brand and we won the pitch.

Due to some logistical problem, we were asked to re-pitch. This was after the client had announced in the media that Ogilvy had been awarded the business. We had won the account based on some very sharp work, and I refused to re-pitch.

Soon after this experience, Kelvinator invited us for a pitch and we tweaked the air-conditioner idea, presented, won the account and were delighted to see our idea later adjudged as the campaign of the year.

Post this campaign, Kevinator's sales, reached levels they had not achieved for many years.

Never throw a good idea away. If you believe in an idea, you might juggle it, you might adapt, you might readjust it. Good ideas are rooted in insights, and good insights are precious. While I do not 'store' them physically, I do 'park' these thoughts in an accessible corner of my brain.

# What is the fastest campaign you've ever done and what was the effectiveness of the campaign?

I would like to start this response with a story. It is a story about Picasso. Picasso was once sitting in a park and a lady came to him and said, 'Can you draw a portrait of mine?' And Picasso said, 'Yes'.

And within a minute, he drew a beautiful portrait of hers with a single stroke and gave it to her.

She said, 'How much do I owe you?'

Picasso answered, '$5000.'

'It took you only a minute,' the lady said.'

Picasso said, 'Madam, it took me my entire life.'

This is a great story that I've heard many of my peers relate, and I love hearing it again and again.

You learn so much over the years from various experiences that, later and unsurprisingly, answers come out so fast that people are not willing to pay you a justifiably high price for the answer.

You're not charging for the time it took you to respond to the question; you're charging for the time it took you to accumulate the knowledge that made it possible for you to answer the question.

But, getting back to my 'fastest' campaign idea.

I've had many 'fast' campaigns in my career, but the one that is closest to my heart is the idea that won us the Bajaj Pulsar account.

A large team from the agency was travelling to Pune for the pitch, armed with five complete campaigns, boarded and finished for the presentation to Rajiv Bajaj and his team. Rajiv had taken on the responsibility of building the motorcycle business.

As was the custom in those times (in the early 2000s), we stopped for breakfast halfway to Pune.

And that's when I had the idea, as we were having our breakfast. The team was discussing the various routes that we had got ready when I interrupted them with, 'We're not going to present these, I have a bigger, better idea.' But we don't have the work,' was the objection. 'That doesn't matter,' was my response, and then I proceeded to share the idea. By the time we reached Bajaj, the whole team was on board and walked in confidently.

The idea was very simple and rooted in a peculiarity found in Indian (and other) languages. All inanimate objects, when referred to in Hindi, have a 'gender'. For example, a chair is feminine. But a chair made of cane and wicker is masculine.

The peculiar attribution of gender is what provoked the thought. Consider this: hefty men in uniform sporting large

moustaches form the bulk of the police force, but in Hindi 'police' is feminine.

There are many such oddities, and I remembered one of them. The scooter, for whatever reason, is masculine, but the seemingly more powerful motorcycle is feminine.

That was the simplicity of the campaign—we would attach a gender to Pulsar, the new motorcycle. Let the category be referred to as female, but the Pulsar, said the campaign thought, was 'Definitely Male'. With due respect to all women, we thought it was perfect. The Pulsar was a sturdy, big motorcycle and, in the language of that era, it was a 'man'.

The idea was thought of at a tea stop, a couple of hours away from the client's office and a couple of hours before the pitch presentation. We left all the finished, beautifully boarded campaigns in our cars and walked in with nothing to show; I carried the idea in my head.

We began our meeting and I told Rajeev, 'Rajeev, I can show you a lot of work which we've left in our cars, but we decided not to because we have a great idea, an idea that will ensure growth for Bajaj.'

He heard the idea and delighted us with his response: 'The agency is definitely new.'

Pulsar was launched as 'Definitely Male'.

And the rest is history.

The question asked of me was, **'What is the fastest campaign you've ever done and what was the effectiveness of the campaign?'**

The effectiveness can easily be seen now. The Pulsar continues, twenty years after its launch, to be the category leader and the mainstay of Bajaj Auto.

When I think about it, I'm not even sure that Definitely Male was my 'fastest' idea for a campaign.

A close contender for the fastest campaign would be the 'Kuch khaas hai hum sabhi me' for Cadbury Dairy Milk. I was on my first international holiday in Hawaii when I received a call from my then boss Ranjan Kapur, because Cadbury wanted to review the account—an account we had worked on for over a decade. I had to abort my holiday plans and book the first flight out. Before I boarded the flight, I had a phone conversation with Ranjan when he shared the brief.

'Kuch khaas hai hum sabhi me', with a girl dancing on the cricket field, was a line I wrote that on the back of a boarding pass on my flight back home.

Was it effective? Almost three decades later, it's still being used by CDM.

## Name a live music concert that you would love to attend/ have loved to have attended?

I would love to have attended a live Beatles concert. I grew up listening to the Beatles, watching Beatles movies and reading whatever little was published on the Beatles those days. I fell in love with their music (I used to sing a Beatles song to myself [the song is 'Don't let me down'; I used to sing it to my bat] as I was batting in cricket), their body language, their personalities and their extraordinary connection with their fans. But the Beatles were a phenomenon at I time that I couldn't dream of a trip abroad, let alone a trip for a concert of the Beatles.

In addition to a Beatles concert, I would have loved to have attended a live concert of Bob Marley for much the same reasons as I listed for the Beatles.

# How do you sell a warm blanket in a city like Chennai?

My only chance is to sell it to the ice sellers who sell ice by the kilo on the roadside, who could use the blanket instead of the gunny sack they use to pack the ice because it's a better insulator. I would probably save the cost of the blanket by the reduction in the ice that melts.

If I'm able to prove that the ice melts less wrapped in a blanket than in the gunny sack, maybe I have a business chance.

# What is the most useless talent you have?

I think I'm quite certain that I'm one of the world's best fluffy omelette makers. But I'm still trying to find the person who trusts me in the kitchen, including my wife. So, I think I'll die with this talent unheralded.

# What would you name your boat if you had one?

I was born and brought up in the desert state of Rajasthan. Consequently, in all my dreams, I've never thought of a boat, let alone naming one that I might own.

The only thing I've named of my own is my home in Goa, the house designed by my wife. I named it 'The Pavilion', because of my cricketing background. Where do you go after a hard day's play? Back to the pavilion. Where do you sit and watch your matches after retirement? You watch them from the pavilion. The pavilion is the resting place for current players and for former players.

If I had a boat, would I have called it *The Pavilion*, because I would have gone there for relaxation? What would I go to the boat for? Would it be to be inspired and get an idea (I've never had an idea on a boat).

It would be to find my peace, to enjoy the atmosphere, to think about the game I'm playing, as cricketers do in the pavilion, so I guess it would be 'The Pavilion'.

## What is the weirdest question that people can ask you?

The weirdest question that has been already asked and answered in the earlier chapter is that how do you maintain your moustache? Do you wax it? Do you comb it? I have no idea how to answer it because I do not maintain, wax or groom my moustache.

# 24

# Memorable Campaigns

Can we say now that polio has been eradicated from India?
What was your role in the polio campaign?

'Eradicated' is the wrong word, India has been declared 'polio-free'.

To be able to say a disease is eradicated, it means 'that **intervention measures are no longer required**, the agent, which previously caused the disease is no longer present'.

In India, intervention measures such as the drops drives are still conducted so that we move towards a day when we will be able to say that polio is 'eradicated'.

So, to answer the full question, many campaigns that I have worked on with my colleagues at Ogilvy have given me joy, delight and pride, but nothing has given me more satisfaction than the polio campaign. 27 March 2014, when India was declared 'polio-free', is etched in my mind.

There was a lot of time spent in creating the campaign by Mr Bachchan, my then colleague Ajay Gahlaut and I. The campaign was created with peculiar constraints; Mr Bachchan was working without a fee and could only give us dates between his other (film) shoots. We managed to convince the noted cinematographer Santosh Shivam to direct the films.

We shot at whichever location where Mr Bachchan was shooting with Santosh, grabbing an hour at lunchtime or half an hour after Mr Bachchan was done for the day.

To compound matters, we were operating on a shoestring budget, needing to call in favours from production partners, so we had to dovetail in their convenience as well.

But all the constraints and difficulty in creating the campaign are forgotten as we think back on the responsibility that we shared in trying to address a gigantic problem.

It all became worth it on 27 March 2014.

Working on the IPL was a different kind of high, a different kind of achievement. How we won the account is a great story. 'Where do you get your ideas from? Is every idea original?'

The brief was very simple; they would like the IPL to be to India like the NBA is to the USA. The format would allow for every team to play four international cricketers, the format would demand that young cricketers were given a chance. So, 'Make the IPL the NBA of India' was the brief.

I had earlier worked with two of my friends, Arun Lal and Amrit Mathur, in creating the original proposal of the

league with Lalit Modi. Being a cricketer for a big part of my life I was hungry about the IPL and, when it came alive a few years later, I was very excited; I wanted Ogilvy to win and handle this business.

And we almost blew our chances to work on the account.

Thanks to an ambiguously worded email, the client expected work to be presented at the pitch, while my interpretation of the mail was that we needed to present only our sporting credentials.

Other agencies invited to the pitch made complete creative presentations.

When our meeting was over, the committee said, 'We expected work.'

I told them that we had misinterpreted the ambiguous email and asked them for an additional twenty-four hours to present creative work and, thankfully, they agreed.

We returned to the office, worried and concerned. For whatever reason, I thought of my father's style of reciting 'Veer Ras', (which translates into English as 'Poetry about bravery').

I sat down in my office and began writing. In a rush, I wrote all the lines—the exact words that became so popular with consumers across the country. It was written in the same style as Veer Ras; about going to take part in a battle, about showing your skills and displaying tour bravery.

When I finished writing the lines, I called up my brother Prasoon who could recite Veer Ras exactly as my father did. Then we contacted Ram Sampath, the music director, and I requested him to cancel everything that he was working on.

My colleagues from Ogilvy, Prasoon and I trooped into Ram's office and began work. After many iterations and inputs from all present, we began recording and, at 2 a.m., we were ready with a scratch, a fantastic song track.

And we went to present the next day to Lalit Modi and a room full of his advisors. Among the advisors was Bharat Patel. Bharat was the one who sent us the mail, the 'ambiguous' mail that caused this situation due to which we had to scramble and create a campaign in twenty-four hours. Bharat and Ogilvy had worked together earlier on Vicks and, at this meeting, he told his colleagues that he had great belief in me and great expectations of me. That set a positive tone before our presentation, and we stepped forward with great confidence.

The presentation done, and we stepped out of Nirlon House (where Lalit had his office) and stepped into Kwality restaurant next door. Kunal Jeswani and I ordered a drink and before we could say 'Cheers', my mobile phone rang. The caller was Lalit Modi, accompanies by his advisors. 'This business is yours,' Lalit said.

I said, 'Cheers' and looked up; I thanked God, thanked my father for his teachings and my brother for making the time and the incredible recitation and thanked Ram Sampath for the flexibility and amazing work.

And I get back to the question asked of me. Was the idea 'original'?

No idea is 'truly' original. Language is not original, life is not original, man elements are not original. But how we put these pieces together is original. When you find a new way to interpret something that already exists, you're being original.

In this case, Veer Ras, the core thought that won is the IPL business, already existed from the days after the great epics were written, thousands of years ago. The interpretation of Veer Ras, connecting the bravery of soldiers to the bravery of cricketers, likening cricket to battle was original.

As has been said many times, when you present something familiar in an unfamiliar manner, that's originality.

To illustrate this further: When David Ogilvy created the 'Man with the Hathaway shirt' ad, the eye patch wasn't something that people had not seen or were not familiar with. But it was unusual to see a man sporting an eye patch in an ad for shirts, and the context made the ad noticeable. David used an everyday item (the eye patch) in an unfamiliar context (a shirt ad) and that's what made people sit up and take notice.

## What is the right price for creativity? Simple question, complex answer.

I've tried to answer this question earlier with Picasso's story. Creativity has been undersold from the moment it got measured by the time seemingly spent on it. There is no price put on the hours, months and years that one might have spent in acquiring the knowledge required to be able to come up with answers in a few minutes.

If you think about it, the electrician, the plumber who visit our house get paid for their knowledge, not the minutes spent. Doctors and engineers get paid for their accumulated knowledge and experience, not for the minutes and hours spent. Until a few decades ago, advertising was paid a royalty till the campaign ran.

For example, a Fevicol ad created in 1993—almost thirty years ago—is still relevant, still works, still delivers. Even after all these years, the ad is run as and when required.

In Fevicol's case, we were compensated by a commission, so it worked well for all. But the same is not true of other clients and other ideas.

As an industry, we must find a better solution to compensation; there are enough instances where an ad runs for more than ten years because it still works. Literally hundreds of crores could have been spent on media to run the ad; we would have received just a one-time payment, which now clients are attempting to link to time 'spent' to arrive at the idea for the ad.

I think we need to start a dialogue again with our clients, with a mutually acceptable metric for measurement. It could be on impact, it could be on results, it could be on duration of the campaign, whatever it is.

But it must change; the current system is just not fair to the creators in advertising.

Some people might not like the statement, but it needs to be said.

Other creative industries have dealt with the problem earlier and dealt with it better.

The music industry is a great example, being paid a royalty on every sale, on every time a song is downloaded or aired. We must look at the best current practices in other industries and convince clients that the current system is broken and needs to be fixed for the benefit of all in the ecosystem.

## How do you deal with open-ended briefs?

It is a brief at Ogilvy that we don't take briefs, we create briefs. Briefs are a result of intense interaction between the client and agency teams.

If clients 'sent' briefs and we just 'received them, it would be like an exchange of letters. They write, we respond. In the communication business, all those involved in the creation of a solution must communicate with each other. The client's business depends on the final brief and the interpretation of the brief; that's why the brief has to be an iterative process that ends when all in agreement that it addresses the business problem that needs to be solved.

The architect's business perhaps illustrates this best. You give the architect a brief; the architect returns with ideas; you discuss the ideas, make some suggestions; these suggestions are incorporated for you to see; you approve them, and the work begins. Finally, you have your dream house.

The starting point of a brief MUST have a degree of open-endedness, but the objective has to be clear and razor-sharp. The more closed it is, the more likely that it will result in hundreds of similar solutions.

Briefs are like a diving board, strong enough and flexible enough to take your weight and allow you to make the dive. While the diving board may be the same, different divers leverage the board differently, allowing them the room to make their own creative expression. The tightness of the brief is important for you to know the destination, in much the same manner that the diving board leads to the pool. How you dive should be left to you and your creativity.

# What are the kinds of questions you might ask about the consumer to get a fresh insight?

At Ogilvy, I'm surrounded by people who are sensitive to consumers who meet consumers. Talking to consumers is not like a census study with close-ended questions. Questions that are close-ended will throw up black and white answers— the grey, the nuance will be missed out. We will not get to know about how the consumer 'feels' instinctively and react instinctively to something.

The best planners or the best creative professionals 'talk' to consumers continuously—simple everyday conversations that unearth their true thoughts, their likes and dislikes, their views on various issues, their reactions to an ad or to an idea.

I'm not at all in favour of asking consumers to answer questionnaires; I've seen company after company go wrong on the basis of such responses. If you ask the same question to a group of ten consumers, the consumer is always trying to figure out what the other nine will feel about the response and tries to arrive at the 'right' answer rather than the honest, 'desired' answer.

# 25

# Celebrities and Advertising

You are not a big fan of using celebrities in advertising.
What caused you to work with Amitabh Bachchan when
Cadbury was in a crisis? Was Bachchan the correct celebrity
for the target audience of women and children?

Getting back to the use of Mr Bachchan, the job we had at that time was not to sell more chocolate; the job was to save the reputation of the company and bring trust back in the company.

Secondly, in the time of the Cadbury crisis, our job was not to sell chocolate immediately; because chocolate was loved, our job was to negate the negativity in the consumer's mind.

We needed a voice of sincerity and honesty to communicate to the people and were convinced that Mr Bachchan was the perfect answer. Before Mr Bachchan agreed, he actually wanted to see what changes had been made, what precautions had been taken, he wanted to see the manufacturing process and be convinced that Cadbury was safe. That is precisely how we wrote the commercial. A doubtful and worried Mr Bachchan at the beginning, moving on to a confident Mr Bachchan who was convinced of all the safety and hygiene aspects of the manufacturing of Cadbury.

Every problem and its solution have to be seen in the context of the situation and that is why Mr Bachchan, considering his stature and his appeal to all audiences, was asked to perform the task of rebuilding the reputation and not to sell chocolate.

With the runaway success of the exercise, it would have been stupid not to use him to sell chocolate, which we did with the next winning campaign, 'Pappu pass ho gaya'.

In the first case, we used Mr Bachchan as himself, to be used for his credibility. In the second, he was an actor who played a fictional character used to market chocolate.

# I think pronouncements about short attention span are humbug.

Why are all the OTT players like Netflix, Amazon Prime, Zee5, Hotstar and Voot investing in episodic content when it seems we live in a digital world with shrinking attention span?

Why are movies still being made? Why are people reading long-form articles? Why are books still being written, sold and read?

Attention span is in the control of the creator. Are you able to hold the attention of the receiver? Are you able to generate curiosity?

This is where I want to talk about storytelling in our history, in an age where we had no 'media'.

In those days, in villages across the country, people used to gather under large trees in the evenings because there was no work after the sunset. Just because work was over for the day, they didn't all go to sleep immediately; they met for conversations, for entertainment.

And some, among every group of villagers, were storytellers. As they narrated their stories to seemingly captive audiences, a good storyteller would provoke the question 'What happened next?' if he paused for too long. This reaction meant that the audience was being held.

Audiences would walk away to their homes if the story flagged or failed to capture their imagination.

So how well you tell a story, how you are able to hold the attention, how you weave engagement, defines the success of the story, not the duration of the story. It has little to do with attention span and all to do with the quality of the story.

Look at the film industry or even the TV industry. They create short trailers of around a minute or promos of twenty to thirty seconds to convince someone to watch the film or TV show, which could be anything from thirty minutes to two hours. Both the trailer/promo and the film/TV show need to work. One is very short content, one, in today's times, is very long-form content.

A recent trend in advertising is to create two-, three- and four-minute films, not because the story needs the duration, but because you CAN. That's ridiculous. It's the legs of the story that should define the duration, not the access and availability of low-cost media. Many brands have used five-to-ten-second commercials (mostly tactical challenges) because the story could be told in that time, and three-minute commercials because the story demanded the three minutes.

Create communication that has the consumer wondering 'what happens next' and wanting to watch more rather than communication that causes the consumer to walk away.

At Ogilvy, we fight for the few extra seconds that we might need to make a good commercial a great one; and it's always the story that defines the duration.

Children have shorter attention spans, researchers say. But children sit and watch long animation films without showing any signs of impatience. Animated films and episodes for children are not short . . .

The only reason they're watched is that the story captivates the child.

## Can you guarantee the success of an ad?

Unpredictability is a way of life, but our outlook for the future makes some obvious assumptions.

You might plan a lunch for next week or a holiday for next summer, but there's no guarantee you'll wake up alive tomorrow morning.

But you plan these things because based on all the inputs available to you, the chances are that you'll still be around.

To be absolutely certain of an outcome is not possible in most situations. Businesses have been launched, businesses have failed. Brands have been launched, brands have failed. All these are launched with considered risk.

Similarly, when you come up with an idea and invest in a campaign, a collection of people including your client, your partners and the client's partners, collectively believe that the idea will work.

That belief is not just a guess; ads are often pre-tested, shown in advance to key stakeholders, shown to focus groups and so on. And yet, some might fail.

Arguably, you could create ads which are guaranteed not to fail, and they would be equally guaranteed not to excite significantly. Great advertising is often a risk. The risk has both a downside and an upside, and investing in such communication means that the collective view of the team involved is that the upside is more likely.

If you don't take risks, then I'm afraid you will be doing dull, boring and predictable work with no gain or mediocre gain.

I've been asked about the superior quality of content in Bollywood films when compared to that of advertising films. Similarly, there's talk of the high number of 'hits' from Bollywood.

A couple of years ago, I read this statement by Madhur Bhandarkar. 'The success rate in the film industry is 0.1 per cent.'

Obviously, something is seriously lacking in the storytelling, else the success percentage wouldn't be as low.

This assumption that all movie makers are greater storytellers is incorrect. There are bad storytellers in movies, and there are bad storytellers in advertising.

And there are good storytellers on both sides.

In a way, advertising is held to account more rigorously. A movie might do well because it becomes popular, and there's no second metric. In advertising, we are measured by another important metric: Did the ad do the job of selling products or services, or was it only 'popular'?

## Work-life balance

Much has been written about the poor work-life balance in advertising; it's a crisis that concerns not just advertising but every profession. Sailors, pilots, health workers, police personnel, doctors, the armed forces, chartered accounts, the pani-puri wallah, all are struggling, in today's fast-paced world, to balance work and life.

All have to find smarter ways of working, rather than working longer hours or working harder.

Many peers I know in advertising seem to find the balance easily and pursue music careers, careers in theatre, hobbies like cycling or running, serious pursuits like cooking or woodworking and so on.

And, simultaneously, they do well at work, achieving milestones, gaining plaudits, getting promoted and earning more.

I'd like to think that I'm one of those who found a healthy balance as well.

How do they manage it?

It boils down to individual prioritization. You have to decide what is worth it and what is not. Is it really necessary to work over the weekend when you could enjoy a break with the family in Lonavala? Is that extra hour that you think you need to spend on preparing for next week's presentation more gratifying than reading a book and having a drink in the available time?

You have to decide; you have to find your own balance. All companies have defined work hours. How come only 20 per cent of the employees are hanging around after the official close of the workday? It's obvious that these 20 per cent have priorities that differ from that of the 80 per cent.

I don't want to simplify the problem—and it is a problem— but I don't think, in most cases, the company or industry is to blame for poor work-life balance. More often than not, it's individual choices.

# What about bosses who call you late at night for meetings or keep you in the office late, or ask you to be in office on a Saturday or Sunday for a meeting?

I think we cannot generalize on the basis of a few people who may be autocratic or are disrespectful of others. Overall, in the organized sector, increasingly, there is little scope for bosses who do not respect the personal time of colleagues.

But beyond rules and the letter of the law, I do think there are many more good managers than poor managers when it comes to respecting time.

Working late on the odd occasion or working on the odd Saturday is informally compensated for by good managers. You're needed to work on a Sunday and the boss gives you the Monday off, and so on.

Often, we are too reticent to make our views known. I'll share one of my early experiences with the late Shunu Sen, the marketing guru from HUL.

He used to organize meetings on Saturdays with his team and the agency team, and I was one of those who were supposed to attend these meetings, however junior I was (this was in 1983, when I was just a year into advertising).

A conflict arose when I, thanks to my background playing Ranji-level cricket, was appointed to take charge of the Ogilvy's cricket team, and all the official matches were played on Saturdays.

I gathered all my courage and went to Shunu Sen. He'd seen me around in a couple of meetings, so he knew who I was. I went and said to him, 'Mr Sen, I need your help. I've been asked to put together a cricket team for Ogilvy and the matches are only on Saturdays, and Ogilvy has never won a match to date, and since I've been a cricketer it's my challenge. I believe you have meetings on Saturdays; I need you to excuse me. I can come to your house on a Sunday morning. I can come at 6 a.m. to make up for my Saturday absence. But please give me permission to miss the Saturday meetings for the next two months.' He looked at me and laughed. 'Boy, do you think you're that important? I can do without you on Saturday. Now go and win the matches.'

If I hadn't asked Shunu Sen and been excused from the meetings, I would probably have attended all those meetings unhappily.

And I could have, and probably would have, complained about the poor work-life balance.

It's the responsibility of a senior to figure out when you're disturbing somebody's life constantly. And it's the responsibility of all employees to figure out whether they can truly justify being regularly late to work and whether it was, indeed, work.

Hanging out with your colleagues and having a couple of drinks at a pub after office hours is not work. Downloading a film on the office broadband connection after office hours is not work. Hanging around at the office till you're eligible for taxi fare home after work is not work.

There are no easy answers. What I can say with confidence is that those who are truly concerned about work-life balance generally find the balance.

# Piyush, what's your idea of a great holiday? What would you do on a great holiday, where would you go? What would you want to do?

I think the list of places that I want to go to for a great holiday is too long and changes continuously.

The first on my list is the north-east of India. For whatever reason, I've never been there.

From conversations with people from the region or with others who have been there, it's become a must-visit for me, the #1 on my list. I have made brief visits to Guwahati, Johrat, and Darjeeling, all connected to work during my first job with a tea company. I need to do a long visit and understand the people, the food, the music, the clothes, the flora and the fauna better.

I hope it's soon.

---

**Parties and five-star hotels. What is it about these places that puts you off?**

I attend all personal events of friends and family, of my own office and events that are important to the industry.

I'm not comfortable in a large gathering of people where I don't know the majority of those present. That's perhaps why I'm not enthusiastic about parties and five-star hotels.

In general, I'm comfortable in small gatherings of like-minded people at settings where the majority is comfortable and at ease.

But my biggest problem with large events and parties is the visual obscenity of food and the way the food is projected. A buffet with a huge choice of food turns me off.

When there's a small party where I am not faced with heaps of food, I'm fine. I'm comfortable with a single-course meal (even a pizza) or at a table where we're ordering a la carte (because food waste is kept to a minimum). I'm uncomfortable at an event that is attended by many people I'm unfamiliar with. These are normally events that I HAVE to attend as part of my job because I represent the company I work for. In such cases, I stay as long as is required to 'mark my attendance' and then make a quiet, early, discreet exit.

I'm more than happy to take a holiday any time in my home state of Rajasthan. Sometimes you want to repeat places which you have loved, so, of course on that list is my own state of Rajasthan. There's a different kind of comfort you get from the known; when everything is familiar, one relaxes more. So that makes for a great holiday destination.

If all of us take it upon ourselves to explore our home states, we would be the richer for the experiences.

South Africa is a place I've been to five to six times, and I can never tire of it. I think safaris are wonderful even if you've experienced it earlier. For tourists like me, it's four to five delightful days of peace and nature. I've never been to South Africa solely for a holiday; I've been there on work and squeezed in a holiday. Perhaps it's time to go there for a holiday and, if required, squeeze in some work.

To me, a holiday is not about museums and galleries and shopping. I'm consumed by looking at and meeting people, looking at the geography (a little bit of history), the culture.

The culture is the most important. I've heard so much about the unique culture of Ireland that it's on top of my bucket list.

Culture to me includes music, food, street performances, perhaps a musical in some cities.

I've seen enough of five-star hotels; I'd rather stay at quaint places, inns and small hotels. Where possible, I stay with friends or relatives rather than check into a hotel, even if I'm on a work visit.

Rather than be guided around by a professional, I try and get someone I know to show me around and to take me to places they visit. In England, for example, a long drive in the countryside, driven by someone you know and who knows the area is both educational and entertaining.

I enjoy the watering holes and small eateries on highways and in small towns; there's so much character in the food, the furniture, the people and the colours I'm exposed to.

# 26

# In a Relationship

How important is relationship building with clients to the long-term business of an agency?

Tata Sky is a great example of a strong relationship made stronger by the experience of working with each other. We had a fantastic relationship with Harit Nagpal when he was at Hutch/ Vodafone, when we did some great work together. And that is the trust and belief and the chemistry that developed in the earlier relationship that helped us do impactful work when we got to work on Tata Sky. Today, Tata Sky is the leading DTH services company in the country.

As an aside, little is spoken or written about organizational memory and knowledge. Ogilvy as an organization has, over the decades of working with Harit, learned so much about his style of operating, the expectations that he has of the agency, the trust he reposes in the agency and so on. Even if one of my colleagues has not been on a team that worked with Harit before, he or she benefits from the 'institutional' knowledge that floats around. Overall, the account is easier to work on. I certainly imagine that this is true for the client as well.

How can I not mention Bharat Puri? Our relationship goes back thirty-three years and across three companies that he's worked in. Today, he's the CEO at Pidilite. Considering that he knows Ogilvy, most of my colleagues and me well, it makes for a relaxed and productive relationship.

In such relationships, bad delivery surprises are rare.

It also makes for the cutting of red tape and for an unusual efficiency. Lots more is done through short phone calls between agency and client. Criticism and rejection are unhesitating (from the client's point of view) and easier to take (from the agency's point of view).

When there is healthy chemistry between the leaders on both sides of the table, it takes away the hesitancy, ego and distrust that could inhibit efficiency on an account.

Let me underline the importance of chemistry and the long-term benefits. Take the case of the chemistry that we share with Shripad Nadkarni. We first met him in the early 1990s when he was the marketing head of Johnson & Johnson consumer products and we were handling Carefree, Stayfree, Band-Aid and Johnson's babycare range. In addition, we handled Savlon, a brand they had just acquired. Together we did superb work, both from a creativity and effectiveness point of view. Out of the blue arose an international conflict issue and we had to part ways. (The parting was memorable; a dozen adults [six from each side] crying and hugging in Apeejay House, Ogilvy's then Mumbai office.) Since this parting, we worked with Shripad when he moved to The Coca-Cola Company and were entrusted with Limca, Fanta, Kinley water and the launch of the leading brand Sprite. After he left The Coca-Cola Company and started his own consultancy, Marketgate, we continue to work with each other TILL today, on brands and assignments that, unfortunately, I am not free to share. Thanks to our mutual experiences, I am confident that Shripad and Ogilvy will work together even in the future.

Ease of the relationship is a significant contributory factor in the work we do on Mondelez, Asian Paints, Pidilite, Unilevers, ITC, Marico, Lava, Pernod-Ricard and so on.

These are clients who own your shower time. The easier the relationship, the more of our shower time the client owns. Let me expand on that.

You don't think of a good friend or of your father, mother, husband, wife or children at appointed times. You think of them anytime during the day.

The same is true of clients who are 'close' to you.

These are clients you think about at odd hours without there being a need for it, and the clients do the same for you. You could be sitting at home, having a drink, reading a book, listening to music or taking a shower, and an idea for a client could strike you, because the client's business problem is like the problem your spouse or child could have and you think about the solution non-stop.

And in such relationships, you own the client's time as well. You can call the client at 6 a.m. because you have an idea that you think will work for the brand. And the client is happy to receive the call and talk about the idea, because the call came from YOU.

While on Tata Sky, I must talk about another benefit. As is common with large industry groups, the group has a 'culture' that all entities absorb. As a result, if you've worked with one company in a group, it becomes much easier to work on a second, and a third and a fourth. With each addition, the agency and the group gain what I referred to as institutional knowledge of each other, making it easier for all team members on both sides to work with each other.

As an organization, we already had considerable exposure to the Tata culture, having worked (or currently working with) Tata corporate, Tata Cement, Tata Salt, Tata Steel and Tata Motors. Beyond individual respect and relationships, we enjoy institutional respect and relationships.

Clients like Harit are easier to work with because of the clarity of thought, purpose and business objectives. They can clearly explain, while rejecting what you thought was a great idea, why the idea doesn't solve the business problem.

There is a diametrically opposite set of clients who give you a virtual blank canvas.

Take our experience with Center Shock (I must add that Ogilvy and Perfetti Van Melle had worked with each other for a considerable time before this product launch), a brand owned by Perfetti.

Sameer Suneja, now the CEO of Perfetti globally, was our client. When we met first to discuss the new product, Center Shock, Sameer, with his then boss Ashok Dhingra, said to us, 'Partner, I think we've made a great product, now give us a great line.'

That was the blank canvas.

And he handed over the product to me and my team—Center Shock—to sample. I chewed on it, and it was so tangy, that my system just shook up for a while. In minutes, I said, 'I have the line for you 'Hila ke rakh dega' (It'll shake you up).

Their response was instantaneous. 'That's a great line. Now while you do the rest of the mass media communications, I'm going ahead with the line, I'm printing labels that say—"Center Shock: Hila ke rakh dega".'

'Do the rest of the mass media communications' was the brief. Of course I'm simplifying it, but this was the way in which the account took wing.

The product—and a creative response to the sampling of the product—started the Centre Shock journey.

Clients like Perfetti encourage spontaneity, initiative and proactivity that lead to ideas beyond advertising ideas—they're often 'growth' ideas.

The Coca-Cola 'Share a Coke' (international) campaign not only increased brand salience, but also measurably increased the sales of Coke.

As the final touches are being applied to this book, we in India, have developed the 'Palat De' campaign for Thums Up (a brand owned by The Coca-Cola Company) which we believe would result in both market-share and top line growth for the brand.

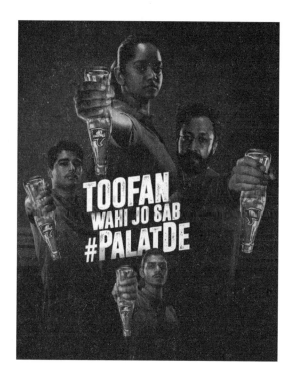

What is common to all these examples? A great relationship of trust between the agency and the brand. Fearlessness to present off-beat ideas to the client. The ability to take criticism and rejection by the agency. Working closely together to develop what seems to be a good idea. Discussing ideas that go beyond advertising.

When you see the benefits of such a philosophy, you wonder why more brands and agencies don't embrace it.

Respect the trust that somebody places in you from day one and always remember to keep the relationship fresh, just like bringing flowers home to your wife (or for your husband).

When Kentucky Fried Chicken (KFC) launched in India, the journey began with a handful of outlets. KFC took a long-term view of India and wanted to study the country before it expanded (they now have over 450 outlets in India). KFC were competing with the samosas and bhaturas, they were competing with substantial meals, marketing a product in a form that was alien to the habits of India.

Their core product, obvious in their name, was fried chicken, entering a country dominated by 'tandoori' chicken.

KFC set itself up for a slow, long and steady journey, confident in its product offering.

Obviously, bridging the culture gap was one of the most important priorities.

The first campaign that we did for KFC attempted to do just that. KFC has invested a fortune on, and built a formidable business with the three words, 'Finger Lickin' Good'.

We had two assets to play with: fried chicken, the product and 'Finger Lickin' Good, the line.

So our first campaign leveraged these two assets with a print and outdoor campaign which only showed a pair of hands and the a line that said, 'Cutlery at KFC: Finger Lickin' Good'.

The ad made a virtue of the common Indian habit of eating with hands (and building on Finger Lickin' Good) and decreased the seeming alienation of a 'foreign' chicken dish.

Two cultures came closer—encouraging consumers to sample the product with more confidence.

That campaign is history and today, KFC marches closer to 500 outlets in India, and gives meaning to the line 'Finger Lickin' Good'.

And it's growing by not remaining static; since the launch in 1995, the KFC menu, while remaining true to the 'Kentucky Fried', has been expanded to include other food that's 'Finger Lickin' Good' like the paneer zinger.

How durable a brand is depends on how the brand image is maintained and refreshed. CEAT Tyres, present in India since 1958, lost their way as they failed to look after their brand. In the early 1980s, the Italian brand was bought by the RPG Group. After taking stock of their brand assets, in the early 2000s CEAT redesigned their marketing structure, launched a new brand identity and infused new life into the brand image. After this exercise, CEAT has been continuously bringing new energy into their marketing with innovative advertising and ad placements.

Like CEAT, Bisleri is another brand that felt the need to refresh. Before multinational water brands like Aquafina and Kinley entered the country, Bisleri enjoyed enviable market-share and became generic to the category; all bottled water was referred to as 'Bisleri'.

While this might be good for the ego, it's not good for business, as consumers would pick up any bottled water and believe that it was Bisleri they were buying.

Bisleri is owned by Ramesh Chauhan, a man who is an authority on the category; the man who created the iconic brands Thums Up and Limca (which he sold to Coca-Cola). We were called in to address this very specific problem. My team and I spent an extraordinary amount of time understanding the specifics of the problem before we presented our campaign to address the challenge.

We presented camels as 'water experts', and Ramesh Chauhan reacted instantly and positively to the thought. These camels are seen in situations when other branded water brands are attempted to be passed off as Bisleri; the camels can't be fooled and reject these attempts and, indeed, school, those who were trying to fool them. The campaign is ongoing, and, as I write this, the brand's market share in a hugely competitive market continues to grow.

Ogilvy India has always looked forward to working with good Indian companies in addition to multinational companies. Companies don't compare our size to theirs; they will always be bigger. Our track record will show that, in addition, we've worked enthusiastically with small brands with small budgets as well, as is evident from our association with Fevicol, which was only a trade brand at the time we took it on.

Maybe the next such brand we work on will be another Fevicol for us.

It's work on brands like Fevicol, Mondelez and Hutch (later Vodafone) that got us noticed by Sunil Raina, the then head of marketing at a then unknown mobile handset brand called Lava. Sunil was a follower and fan of all Ogilvy work.

At a conference, he walked up to Anant Rangaswami (the curator of this book) and requested an introduction to me. Anant set up the meeting, and we've been working with Lava ever since.

Sunil was transparent about the size of their company, the modest budget and their ambitions; we've worked with these parameters in mind and, together, have created work that has worked for Lava.

Don't turn away seemingly small clients.

1. They might be wonderful clients—clients that your teams are delighted to work with
2. Their ambitions might not be reflected in their current size
3. Their product could add to the diversity of the categories you work on, which is always a good thing

Lava ticks all the boxes, and, in Sunil, I have another friend.

If ignoring new Indian brands is to ignore large opportunities, under-resourcing 'network' clients is another commonly committed error because these businesses are seen as 'safe'.

Castrol is one such brand, and we ensure that we resource them well and that our teams are truly committed to the brand. We wanted to do great work on the brand so that, at international Castrol marketing conferences, our work would be discussed. (Our work for HUL's brands always gets discussed and often wins awards at Unilever's internal conferences; this has become a benchmark for us.)

Castrol, like any lubricant, sees the major business coming from the truck segment. There is no way international ads could be repurposed for the Indian market, so we began a process of making Castrol an international brand that truly understands India. While successive mass media campaigns have been released over the years to build the brand, special efforts have been made to connect to the primary influencer— the truck driver.

We created twenty-one specially curated yogasanas (exercises) for truckers, in an attempt to help them stay fit and healthy.

And, in the process, the international Castrol gets closer to Indian truckers.

You've spent thirty-nine years in this
business. Who would you award as the
best client you've ever had in your life?
An individual, not a company or team.

I've had the luxury of having many great clients, who helped
me develop as a professional, who helped me develop as an
individual, who helped me, and Ogilvy succeed. But if I had
to name ONLY one client who contributed the most to my
development, that client would be Madhukar Parekh of Pidilite.

My relationship with Madhukar Parekh has been almost
as old as my relationship with Ogilvy—just short of thirty-nine
years now. Madhukar Parekh is a visionary, a man with high
respect for his partners and collaborators, a man who doesn't
talk about his extraordinary contribution to society through
his philanthropic activities, a man who has stayed as humble
and understated as he was on the day I met him, despite his
company having grown by a factor of thousands since then.

He's generous in his praise (perhaps over-generous) and a
joy to work with always. He, and his family, are like family
today to me (and my family).

So, here's the one name: Madhukar Parekh.

Imagine if someone had the power to give
you, no questions asked, the account of your
choice. Which is the one account that you
would want to win as global CCO of Ogilvy?

In addition to the wonderful clients that Ogilvy has globally
and in India, I would love to work on Apple. It's a brand I

admire, a brand that I use every day and, if its advertising and marketing is anything to judge, it's a brand that understands and embraces creativity and invests in the power of creativity. In India, I would love to work with a brand from Mahindra & Mahindra. I've been associated with Anand Mahindra to a small extent through my involvement in the Indian Pro Kabaddi League, but I've never had Anand as a client. I don't care if it's an unexciting category or one of their smaller businesses, I'd love to work with Anand Mahindra.

# 27

# My Inspiration

Can you name the person who has had the greatest impact on your life?

Without a doubt, that person is my mother.

My mother because hers is the story of somebody who was so evolved in so many ways.

Consider her life: She was born in a village; she did not get the privilege to study beyond a point and got married, as was the custom of those times, at an early age. She read whatever was available in the house and improved her reading and her 'education' through dint of application and conviction.

Whatever she could not actualize, she tried to achieve through her (nine) children. With the obvious and necessary support of my father, she ensured that all my sisters were well educated (not so common in those days) and were encouraged to pursue their interests despite pushback and criticism from well-meaning relatives and family friends.

If she was told that something could 'not be done', her answer was a firm, 'Why shouldn't we do it? I trust my children to be responsible and careful.'

She actively encouraged one of my sisters to travel to the Netherlands to study film direction and film production (she got a scholarship) in the 1970s! Here she was, sending an unmarried girl abroad; eyebrows were raised. My mother would have none of it. My sisters, between them, are doctors, singers, theatre actors, writers, historians, news readers, teachers, and all of them got their foundations from the support and encouragement of my mother.

My mother fully supported my dalliance with cricket and my brother's ambition to pursue an education in design at the National Institute of Design (NID).

All of us siblings are what my mother allowed us to become.

There's a mystery that all of us siblings have never been able to solve. While it was always apparent that money was difficult to come by at home, how could my parents be so generous all the time?

We were a large family of eleven; including our house help, we were thirteen or fourteen. Yet, my mother's house was always available for anyone who needed a roof over their head; relatives of relatives stayed at our house from time to time as they came from smaller towns to pursue their education in Jaipur.

So much generosity, sharing what little we had was something my mother pulled off, but we never felt that we were short of anything.

My mother was the personification of generosity and of self-confidence. To illustrate, she was summoned by the principal of my school who wanted to draw her attention to my misbehaviour in class. Tired of being summoned repeatedly, she told him one day, 'Listen, I have other children to look after and a house to run. Between 9 a.m. and 3:30 p.m., he is your responsibility. If he misbehaves and you want to punish him, please do so but you cannot punish me.

She understood diversity and gender equality instinctively and, as a result, all the siblings have imbibed the understanding. None of the nine children she had felt that he or she was the favourite; none received less attention than the other. All the daughters were encouraged to study to the level that they wanted to, and all became graduates or postgraduates. When faced with a daughter wanting to marry a Muslim, my mother, within the scope of societal constraints, supported the decision.

She was also the greatest bonding agent, holding the larger family together in unity. If I travelled somewhere, she would give me a list of names, addresses and phone numbers, saying, 'Oh, you're going to Calcutta? Buy a box of sweets and go and meet X.'

I'd say, 'But who is X?'

And she'd say, 'She's your father's close friend's relative. And try and meet Y, who is a distant cousin. If you can't go because it's too far or you don't have the time, then definitely make a call saying that you were in town.'

And she'd encourage all of us to keep in touch with our relatives, our friends. Calls saying, 'Do not forget it is your brother-in-law's birthday day after tomorrow,' were routine.

There was something about her that made a big impact on anyone who met her, despite the language barrier (she wasn't proficient in English). On one occasion, Ogilvy's entire global creative council visited Jaipur for a conference. I mentioned to Robin Putter, then worldwide creative head, who was my boss at that time, that I was from Jaipur and that my mother still lived in the city. Robin immediately said that he wanted to meet her. Soon, the entire council wanted to come to meet my mother, a woman they had heard so much about.

My mother was ageing in those days. She used to walk around the house, she used to do the housework, but she didn't go out much, as she was conscious in public places.

So, I suggested to Robin, 'Why don't all of us go home and meet her? It's a small house, so some can hang about in the garden, and some can meet her and sit with her.' The entire team agreed. Since there was no alcohol in my house, we took bottles of wine and alcohol and borrowed glasses from the hotel and took it home.

It was a most unusual afternoon in the course of an advertising conference, but an afternoon that is remembered by all who attended, thanks to their interaction with my mother.

For years, the first question I would be asked by anyone who was there that evening was, 'How is your lovely mother? What news of your home?'

Colleagues still talk to me about their memories of the visit to my mother's house.

That's the kind of impact she had on people.

People used to gravitate to her; she was a people magnet. Strange people used to come to my house, and say, 'I've just come to say a quick hello and have a cup of tea with her.' They would talk about their problems with her, and she would make her humble suggestions and they would eventually leave, happier for having spent time with my mother.

That ramble was to answer a short question on who has impacted me the most. Perhaps it's because I haven't spent as much time with others and haven't been exposed to the various factors that contribute to making them whole as my mother.

To the younger lot of those who might read this book— look inside your home; look into your childhood and you will find many answers. Like I did.

# 28

# From Jaipur to Delhi to Mumbai to Goa

Here is a very interesting question, especially the source of the question. How did I move to Goa? How have I adapted to Goa?

This question is from a woman called Anjula Bedi, who is family to us. She was a classmate of one of my sisters in Jaipur and our two families have been close ever since.

Anjula's late husband Satish Bedi was the one who introduced me to Ogilvy. Ranjan Kapur and Satish Bedi were friends, and, when requested by Satish, Ranjan agreed to interview me.

As I began this book, Anjula heard about it and wanted me to answer how I was dealing with moving to Goa and how I occupied myself in Goa. While Nita and I have owned the house in Goa for more than ten years, my stays in Goa have never been longer than a month. I've now been here continuously from March 2020, save for a short trip to Mumbai.

In Goa, we live off the beaten path in a small village called Guirim. It's a quaint little village far from the main city with hardly any traffic, and not even a single shop in the actual village. I have plenty of trees around me and birds chirping through the day. The ambience is uncluttered, encouraging me to think, to write, without being disturbed by noise or interruptions. It also encourages me to do things I haven't done before, like pottering around in the garden and learning to identify different birds.

Being stuck here, I've been forced to adopt the basics of technology and stay connected with work continuously. So, I've had the best of two worlds: a profitable work day while staying in serene Goa. There are things I do in Goa that I could never imagine doing in Mumbai, such as a two-hour drive without encountering a traffic jam. I had hardly stepped out of the house for some months because of lockdown and restrictions when close friends, the Pinto de Rosaarios, said to me, 'You've been sitting at home for a long time. Let's go for a picnic.' The couple picked me up (they had lunch and coffee packed for us) and drove to parts of Goa that I had never seen. Goa is cliché-ridden and needs a prod from friends for you to be exposed to the beautiful underbelly.

The world knows about Goa's beaches, its chilled-out life, its shacks, Goan food and its churches. But during the pandemic, when I spent an extended period of time in my village, I enjoyed the beauty of observing farmers and farming at close quarters, of seeing bullocks being used in the farming, of marvelling at how organized the farmhands are when the paddy is being sown and when the paddy is being harvested.

I was fascinated to see egrets chasing tractors to hunt for the worms that are forced to the surface thanks to the ploughing. Hundreds of egrets appear, as if from nowhere, as the tractor operator guns the engine and form a procession flying in hope of a good meal.

A hornbill in my courtyard, golden orioles all over, a kingfisher that arrives the same time every morning as I sip on a cup of tea. This long stint in Goa has taken me back in time, to a time when visits to villages were common and birdsong was everywhere. Goa, for me, is a continuous reminder that there is an India beyond the cities, a beautiful India.

# Afterword

Having undergone this exercise of attempting to answer questions from all of you, I can easily understand how Chajju had the patience and discipline to do this every day.

Because he gained from the exercise, as I did.

You entered the chaubara and asked me your questions; I had to dig deep to find the answers that were useful to you. In the process, I had to think afresh about advertising and my experiences, asking myself why I did something or the other in some particular way or another.

So, the answers to you enriched me as well; they were answers to me and for me.

So, I thank you all for visiting the chaubara.

And that led me to think of all the chaubaras that I've visited, and kept visiting, during my life when I was in search of answers . . .

The one I've visited for the longest time is Major Bhooth ka chaubara. Major Bhooth (as friends fondly call him, is actually Anil Kumar) who is my friend from when we were in Class 1. We worked together in our first jobs as well, and his chaubara is one I visit when I want answers on anything that pertains to nature. Bhooth was a tea-planter by profession who retired early to live in his father's farm outside Jaipur. While not being an expert on nature, he is certainly an aficionado.

Arun Lal ka chaubara, increasingly, is one that I visit almost every day, on the phone or through WhatsApp. Arun has all the answers on resilience and fighting back, first seen by me when he was my rock in the days when he was my captain in the cricket team at St Stephens. I turn to him when I need a dose of courage, of strength. His fighting spirit is best seen in his battle with a rare form of jaw cancer for over six years a battle he won. After this setback, only someone like Arun could bounce back to coach the Bengal cricket team, which is a responsibility he shoulders today.

## Tony aur Mony ka Chaubara

Two brothers, Amitabh (Tony) and Amrit (Mony) Mathur have been friends from our school days. Both competent officers in the civil services, they are retired now but the goodwill that they enjoy will keep them rich forever. I have never seen anyone (or any two) who enjoy the love and respect of all who have met them. Between them, their goodwill keeps them connected to anyone in administration in India. When I enter their chaubara, I can expect to receive solutions to any problem that I might place before them.

## Doc ka Chaubara

He's not quite my local doctor. Dr Bijoy Apte gave up his lucrative private practice to open a clinic in Panchgani because it was an under-served area. He's my go-to person for all health issues, be it a niggle in my calf or a feeling of breathlessness. Doc doesn't treat me; he listens patiently to my description of the complaint and recommends doctors who he thinks appropriate. I've never paid him a fee, because that's not what Chajjus like Doc would expect.

## Indrangan ka Chaubara

Indrangan is the name of the family house created by my late parents. In their lifetime, it was the source of answers to life, the universe and everything.

Today, I visit the chaubara to seek answers from my sisters and my brother on the widest possible range of questions. How much hing (asafoetida) should be added in kali dal? Who is the greatest classical Hindustani flautist alive? Does this script sound believable? What should I wear for a reception at Rashtrapati Bhavan? Do you know a good diabetologist in Bengaluru?

Indrangan ka chaubara has all the answers, served with generous portions of love.

## Now we come to Jaipur ka Chaubara

I was born in Jaipur, so Jaipur ka chaubara taught me how to crawl, to walk, to run. I keep returning to learn of the changes in the environment, in culture, the arts and in the kachodi at Koteta's little shop.

## And the next stop, Nita ka Chaubara

Right now, I'm in Nita ka Chaubara. More precisely, I'm in the drawing room our house designed by my wife Nita in

---

Guirim, Goa. Astonishingly (because I've never noticed this earlier), it's got doors and windows on all four sides. Nita's been my sounding board on all things, including advertising. She's got all the answers to my questions on dogs and other animals, food, culture, music and movies.

And of course, my health, my happiness and my equanimity.

## Finally, we visit late Harnarayan Pandey ka Chaubara

Our uncle, who was like a grandfather to us siblings, was a lettered and erudite man who wrote a book called *Chajju ke Chaubara Me* in the 1950s. This book, written for the rural population, helped them understand concepts of science such as electricity, the telephone, how railway engines worked, the cinema and so on, illustrated through 154 simple images. I learnt many things from him, the most useful being the knowledge of the existence of Chajju and his experiences.